Wienerschnitzel

Wienerschnitzel: The Family Recipe for Success is published under Aspire, a sectionalized division under Di Angelo Publications, Inc.

Aspire is an imprint of Di Angelo Publications.
Copyright 2022.
All rights reserved.
Printed in the United States of America.

Di Angelo Publications
4265 San Felipe #1100
Houston, Texas 77027

Library of Congress
Wienerschnitzel: The Family Recipe for Success
ISBN: 978-1-955690-02-7

Words: John Galardi, JR Galardi
Cover Illustration: Provided by The Galardi Group, Inc.
Cover Design: Savina Deianova
Interior Design: Kimberly James
Lead Editor: Cody Wootton
Editors: Ashley Crantas, Willy Rowberry, Theresa Silvester

Downloadable via Kindle, NOOK, iBooks, and Google Play.

For educational, business, and bulk orders, contact sales@diangelopublications.com.

1.Business & Economics --- Entrepreneurship
2. Business & Economics --- Corporate & Business History
3. Business & Economics --- Development --- Business Development
4. Biography & Autobiography --- Business

Wienerschnitzel

THE FAMILY RECIPE FOR SUCCESS
FROM HOT DOG TO TOP DOG

JOHN GALARDI
JR GALARDI

ABOUT THE GALARDI GROUP

Based in Irvine, California, Galardi Group is the parent company to restaurant brands including Wienerschnitzel, the world's largest franchised hot dog chain, as well as Hamburger Stand and Tastee-Freez.

This book reveals the history of Galardi Group's founder and his son, illuminates an example of how a family-owned business succeeded from one generation to the next, and gives a glimpse into the bright future of the company. This is the tale of a legacy built from the ground up within the walls of a family-owned restaurant chain that grew to impact people from around the world.

CONTENTS

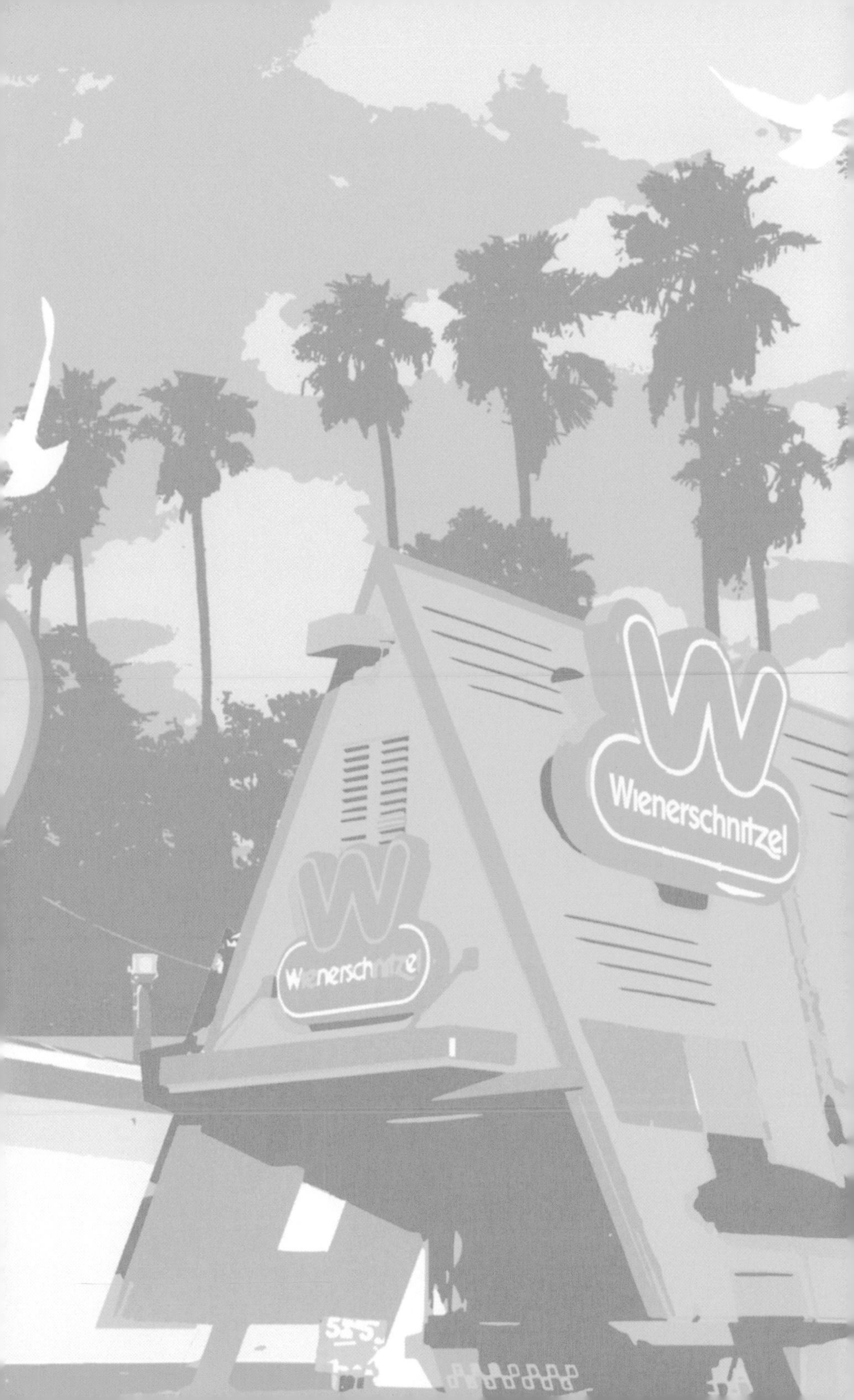
Wienerschnitzel

PART
ONE

Laying the Foundation

John Galardi was a visionary and a man like no other. Against all odds, he managed to build the largest hot dog chain *ever*. The company he started in 1961, with the unusual name and iconic red roof, left an undeniable imprint on the American landscape. Through Wienerschnitzel, he created jobs and entrepreneurial opportunities for thousands of people. He also established a dependable place where families and friends could come together and enjoy each other's company, as well as some fun food. As John used to say, "Who doesn't like hot dogs?"

John didn't much like talking about himself. He would rather hear what you had to say, which is a rare and humbling quality. He did, however, enjoy speaking off-the-cuff wherever he was, even at large franchisee conventions. He'd read the audience and temper his remarks to the atmosphere in the room. In corporate brainstorming sessions, he liked the give-and-take of ideas among his management team. And when everyone was done sharing, he'd say, "Well, here's the deal." That was the signal to everyone listening that John had the game plan fixed in his head.

His desktop at the office was immaculate. He must have believed that an uncluttered desk leads to an uncluttered mind. And that rang true of John's thinking. He had an uncanny ability to focus, and to "cut to the chase." He would identify where an opportunity or a problem lurked, and like an agile basketball player (which he still was, into his forties), he'd grab the ball, run with it, and score.

***

John Galardi grew up very poor in rural Missouri, and when he was nineteen, his family decided to seek their fortune in California. The first thing they did was hit the ground running in their search for employment. Unfortunately, the Eisenhower Recession temporarily slowed job opportunities, even in California. The desirable jobs the Galardis dreamed of didn't materialize as quickly as they had hoped. Within a few weeks, though, Ross (father), Virginia (mother), and Phil (brother) had all managed to find some kind of work.

John was not as lucky and still on the search. For days, he knocked tirelessly on door after door up and down Colorado

Boulevard, looking for a job. He never lost faith and remained determined and optimistic that every no was one step closer to a yes.

Then one day, just as the hot sun was setting over Colorado Boulevard, John walked past Taco Tia, the precursor to the better-known Taco Bell. A man named Glen Bell owned the Mexican fast-food stand in Pasadena, as well as a number of locations in San Bernardino. It seemed this most recent addition in Pasadena was off to a rocky start. Bell was apparently facing difficulties that he hadn't experienced in his other stores, including finding quality employees. Minimum wage was the going rate, and out of the fifty people who applied for a job, none of them met Glen's standards of an ideal candidate.

On that particular day at dusk, there was a woman outside hosing down the parking lot. About to give up on his search and go home for the night, in a last-ditch effort, John called out to her, "You lookin' for any help?" The woman happened to be Glen Bell's wife, Marty. She worked right alongside her husband, taking care of the books and general business matters, so she was very well aware of the difficulty they had been having trying to find responsible workers. After taking a look at John, she sized him up as a presentable young man.

"What kind of work are you looking for?" she asked.

He smiled back. "Anything you got."

John was bright and eager, the exact qualities the Bells were finding so hard to come by in their employees. Marty wasted no time leading the way inside.

John was hired on the spot and started the very next day as a part-time janitor making fifty cents an hour. Though the pay wasn't ideal, it was the start he'd been searching for. With his confident nature and ebullient personality, John knew he wouldn't remain a minimum-wage employee very long. What he didn't know was that this chance encounter would change his life forever.

True to his word, John was willing to do any kind of work required. He cleaned everything spotlessly and would stay well past closing hours to make sure the taco stand was in tip-top shape. Not only was John a hard worker, he also wanted to learn everything Glen Bell had to teach. Glen recognized that John was special, and he was happy to share what he knew. In the hours after the store closed, John and Glen often hung out together to talk about everything fast food, as well as Glen's vision for expanding the Taco Tia brand. John wasn't shy about throwing his own unique ideas into the mix. Glen recognized the great potential in John, and the two men developed a close bond.

Besides being a good businessman, twenty-nine-year-old Glen Bell was also a great showman and marketer. He was known for staging elaborate store openings with mariachi bands, dancers, and banks of klieg lights sweeping the night sky. He also offered coupons and giveaways for a Taco Tia bargain. He passed on invaluable secrets about the industry to John: for example, have your friends park their cars in the lot next to the restaurant to make it look busier than it is, and the colors most apt to stimulate a customer's appetite are red and yellow. Perhaps the most important lesson John learned from Glen, though, was that customers wanted high-quality food and service that was not only fast, but also friendly and personable. John often heard customers comment on the good quality and low prices of the food, but the key to success was about much more than that. John understood that the speedy service and the servers' bright smiles and eager-to-please attitudes kept customers coming back to Taco Tia.

Despite the slow start at the Pasadena Taco Tia, Glen's business was thriving elsewhere. He was also involved with three other partners in a new chain of stores under the name of El Taco. John quickly saw that Glen Bell and his peers in fast food were on the cutting edge of a booming industry. Several factors were prompting this surge in the fast-food business. One was that teenage boys wanted cars, which meant they needed to work. Part-time fast-food work while they were still in school was ideal, so these teens made the hiring pool huge.

Marketers and advertisement agencies jumped on this development. Their ads featured cute girls adorning cool cars and touted burgers and drinks. They brilliantly paired the fast-food industry with California's car culture. It became cool to eat on the go. Also, women were joining the workforce and often didn't have time to prepare a home-cooked meal. It was convenient for all.

As the months went by, John observed Glen even more intently. He saw that he was always focused on the bottom line and how to make his business ventures more profitable. After all, it always came down to profit in the end. Glen recognized that servers in the individual stores spent too much time cleaning and cutting up vegetables, so he decided to open a central commissary where the bulk of the prep work could be handled by a small crew. The food would then be shipped to the Taco Tias and El Tacos in and around Los Angeles. The concept was solid, but the cost savings were negligible, mainly because the commissary was poorly run. Glen knew he needed a responsible employee to manage the entire commissary operation for it to work. John thought that was a great idea, especially when Glen asked him if he would take over the job—with a pay raise. Of course, he jumped at the chance to get a weekly salary and rise from the ranks of the hourly minimum wage.

That promotion put John on the fast track to fulfilling all his promises to Myrna, his fiancé, who was finishing school in Missouri. By the time she graduated from Southwest Baptist College, John had a steady, responsible job with upside potential that paid an unheard-of $150 per week. He rented an apartment in Pasadena for him and his bride-to-be and sent Myrna a one-way train ticket to California. At last, they began planning their wedding. They had made it through the distance and obstacles, and the pieces were finally all in place.

Within a year of John's promotion, Glen Bell had moved him from the commissary and installed him as the manager of his Taco Tia in Long Beach. Myrna was excited for the move, mainly because it meant John wouldn't come home every night smelling of chopped onions. With the move, there also came another shift. It seemed that between the Taco Tias and the rapid expansion of all the new El Tacos, Glen Bell suddenly found himself in over his head financially. Glen needed capital to open several new stores—and he needed it fast.

He knew that John had been carefully saving his money, so he asked John if he could borrow $6,000 with the promise he would repay John $9,000 within three months. John was happy to help Glen out but insisted he would take only the $6,000. Three months came and went, and Glen was unable to pay back the debt, so he had to make a radical business decision. He came up with the idea to turn the Long Beach Taco Tia over to John for a bargain price of $12,000. The terms were that John would pay off the additional $6,000 as a loan, after which the stand would belong to John. He accepted Glen's offer immediately. The Galardi family celebrated the amazing news along with an additional development: Myrna was pregnant and soon had their first child, Teresa.

Now that John was a father, his own boss, and finally making real money, he thought it was time to really settle into the new life he was building. He found a quaint house for his new family in Wilmington for $19,000. When John told Myrna about it, he had, in fact, already purchased it. Making monumental decisions and then telling his wife after the fact would become a pattern in John's life. He believed he was doing what was best and that she would go along with whatever decision he made. Right or wrong, that was how things were.

Though the new house was a shorter commute to the Taco Tia than their old home, John was gone a great deal. He was often at work from 8 a.m. until closing at 10 p.m. The long hours and responsibility were a lot for anyone to handle, even someone as motivated as John. Most of the customers worked at the nearby oil refinery and at businesses along the Pacific Coast Highway, but not every patron was that breed. There was always a group of rowdy kids who'd park their cars in the Taco Tia lot. They would order one taco and spend the rest of the evening being menaces. One night, a particularly irritating kid stuck his head through the order window and carved his initials on the side of John's brand-new cash register. John wasn't one for confrontations, even though he was physically fit and could have easily taken the kid down in a fight. That wasn't his style. John was much too cool and collected for that. He simply took a knife from the kitchen, went out to the parking lot, and carved his initials on the hood of the kid's car. Let him explain that to his father!

That night, when he finally made it home, Myrna could see the exhaustion in John's eyes. After relaying the unpleasant incident, John just shook his head and said, "Maybe I should have become a basketball coach." It was a lament he would often invoke when things weren't going well. Once the dust settled, though, he would refocus on the positive.

At work, Glen Bell kept a close eye on John and watched him make a success of the Long Beach Taco Tia. Since the store was part of Glen's brand, John's success was his success as well. Glen had purchased an empty lot in Wilmington, in a working-class neighborhood at 1326 Pacific Highway. It was about five miles from the Long Beach Taco Tia and a straight shot down the Pacific Coast Highway, which was a major artery that connected one beach town to another. Glen had intended to help his father-in-law open a fast-food restaurant on the lot, but when that didn't pan out, Glen had another idea.

"How would you like to open your own restaurant on a piece of land I own in Wilmington? I'll help you just so long as you stay away from tacos," Glen proposed. And just like that, the deal was done. Glen would lease the land to John, and a handshake would seal the deal (there'd be no formal written agreement). Glen made it clear that he'd help John in whatever way he could, but it was up to John to put together the financing and come up with a new fast-food concept. To help get him started, Glen introduced John to Macy Coffin. At the time, Coffin had established a reputation as the number-one builder of successful fast-food restaurants in California. He'd built stands not only for Glen Bell, but also for many famous sports figures who were investing their hefty paychecks in the fast-food business. Macy was an interesting fellow and a powerful guy who handled every aspect of construction. One day, when some of his workers were arguing about how to lift a heavy piece of machinery onto the roof of a stand they were building, Macy hoisted it on his shoulders, climbed up the ladder, and exclaimed, "Now that's how you do it!" Obviously, he was John's kind of guy. So the two men went into business together.

Macy would put up the $15,000 it would cost to build a stand, in exchange for 6 percent of the gross profits. John grabbed the deal, but there was still one huge unanswered question: What should he sell? McDonald's and In-N-Out Burger had cornered the hamburger market. KFC was selling fried chicken like hotcakes, and tacos or Mexican food were off-limits. Sunny Southern California was, after all, the epicenter of the fast-food industry. Glen suggested, "You know, I did well with hot dogs at one of my first ventures in San Bernardino. What about hot dogs? They're cheap and easy to prepare, you don't need cutlery, and they're popular with adults and kids. They could be a real winner. And no one is doing hot dogs in a big way."

That was the answer! Glen's logic quickly sold John on the idea of hot dogs. It was new and fresh—just what he was looking for. The next order of business was the name. A catchy name is crucial in fast food. He and Myrna hunkered down and brainstormed for days without success. "What about John's Hot Dogs or Wonderful Hot Dogs?" They were officially stumped, until one evening, they were having dinner with Glen and Marty Bell. Marty said, "I was looking through a cookbook today and saw a recipe for Wiener schnitzel. How about that? It's got wiener in it, which is another word for frankfurter."

At the time, everyone thought it was a terrible idea.

Someone said, "Wiener schnitzel is a breaded veal cutlet, and who would even know how to pronounce it? I can't imagine anyone asking, 'Where's the nearest Wiener schnitzel?'"

Two days later, while John was driving around looking at restaurant signs, still struggling to find the right name, he recalled something he'd learned in a marketing class at Southwest Baptist College. When people hear a brand name that sounds familiar, they think, *Oh yeah, I know what that is,* then dismiss it. But when they hear a name that they don't know, it catches their attention, and their curiosity is piqued. They ask themselves, *What's that? Hmm, I'll have to find out.* John ran the idea by a few friends who all also thought "Wienerschnitzel" was a terrible name. So, just like that, John knew it was the right choice. That would turn out to be the way that John made many of his important decisions.

He would test out an idea on other people and then end up trusting his own gut instead. Oftentimes it was contrary to everything he heard.

The name was good, but it still wasn't perfect. John felt that it needed a little something extra. So he added *Der* in front of *Wienerschnitzel.* Technically, it's grammatically incorrect in German, but since he liked the sound of it, he trusted his gut yet again—and Der Wienerschnitzel was born. How Der Wienerschnitzel got its memorable name makes for a fun story to this day and has been the target of good-natured jokes over the years. You can't say "Der Wienerschnitzel" without smiling.

With the name and featured item on the menu firmly in

hand, John had other problems to solve. Most pressing was finding a way to pay for the opening costs. He could think of no people better to turn to first than his basketball buddies.

After a game and over some beers, he asked, "Anyone got five thousand dollars they can loan me?" Predictably, they laughed. Like John, they all had families to support and were struggling to pay the bills they already had, so they hardly had that kind of money individually—or collectively—to loan him. He still had to try. Undaunted, he pushed forward and asked literally everyone he knew.

Unfortunately, he kept coming up empty-handed.

***

He considered getting a bank loan, but he knew he didn't have the collateral now that Myrna was a full-time stay-at-home mom and they were living on one paycheck. Reluctantly, John turned to the two people he least wanted to ask.

Ross and Virginia were both working steady jobs for Sears, Roebuck and Co. While their paychecks did not allow them much in the way of luxuries, their credit was good. Supportive of their son as always, they secured a bank loan on his behalf. John promised his parents that he would pay the loan off as soon as he could, and that was good enough for them. They knew that John's word was his bond.

Now that he had the money to get started, John met

with Macy to approve the architectural plans for Der Wienerschnitzel. These were pretty standard blueprints for the kind of stands that Macy had been building, which weren't original enough for John. He wanted the stand to have a drive-thru window. At the time, the drive-thru concept was a novelty in the fast-food business. There were only a few stands with that feature in all of California, but John knew that the drive-thru was imperative. It was going to solve a number of customer- and service-related problems he had identified working at the Taco Tia. He knew from firsthand experience about rowdy teenagers who liked to hang around the parking lot. John figured if people could order from their cars, pay, and drive away with their food, he could maintain better control of the environment and handle more customers in less time. Macy thought it was a simple fix and modified the blueprints by dividing Der Wienerschnitzel into two small buildings separated by enough space for a car to drive through. The front building housed the order window and the kitchen, and the back building held the supply room, walk-in refrigerator, and office. Construction was completed in just three months, in June 1961, and came in on budget, with Macy at the helm and John overseeing its progress.

During construction, John was busy at work on the rest of his lengthy to-do list: signage, uniforms, kitchen equipment, and supplies. He also kept in mind the adage of "Keep it simple, stupid" in regard to the menu. A work in progress, it would have only three types of hot dogs—with either mustard, chili, or sauerkraut—

and soft drinks. Hot dogs were fifteen cents and drinks were ten cents, right in line with competitive fast-food prices. A unique recipe for chili, which would be Der Wienerschnitzel's "special sauce," was also important to John, to further set him apart from the pack. Once again, John turned to his mentor, Glen Bell, who had years of experience developing the Mexican chili recipe they used at Taco Tia. He and Marty assured John that he only needed to adapt their original recipe by adjusting the Mexican spices in order to cook up a tasty chili that would go well with hot dogs. After an endless evening of making one pot of chili after another, adding, removing, and adjusting ingredients to each trial batch, they finally came up with the winning recipe that everyone agreed was delicious.

With everything falling into place and the grand opening of Der Wienerschnitzel only days away, anticipation was at a high. To add to the excitement, Myrna announced she was pregnant again! A new chapter was about to commence.

John contemplating the next big thing, 1960s.

Finding the X Factor

2

1961 was an aspirational year for the entire country. It started with the inauguration of the young and dynamic John F. Kennedy, which filled Americans with hope. In May, astronaut Alan Shepard blasted off into space in the *Freedom 7*. From liftoff to reentry, the entire mission lasted just fifteen and a half minutes, but it further galvanized the country and set the United States on a course to win the space race against the Soviets. Kennedy pledged that we would have a man on the moon before the end of the decade. The country was running on high. Young Americans were dreaming big, right along with their young president. His movie-star good looks and display of World War II heroism made him an inspiration to young men. John caught the fever of optimism that the president was spreading and ran with it.

On July 5, 1961, the day before Der Wienerschnitzel opened its doors, John worked through the night. He reluctantly left the store after obsessing over every detail just before the dawn's early light broke through the darkness. All the kitchen equipment was tested; the counters, floors, and every inch of the store were thoroughly cleaned; the supplies and paper goods were organized; and the hot dogs, buns, mustard, and sauerkraut were all ready to go. The only task left was to cook the chili, the "special sauce." He decided to leave it until morning so that it would have that freshly made taste. After an internal debate about leaving, he managed to get home with barely enough time to grab a quick nap, take a shower, and head back for the big day.

John came home to find Myrna and their daughter, Teresa, nestled together, and when he left before 6 a.m., they were still sleeping. As he drove through the empty streets of Wilmington, the rising sun rimmed the gray morning clouds in pink and gold.

John took it as a good omen, which was just what he needed. For days, he'd tortured himself with imagining one disastrous scenario after another: he would come back to discover the store had been broken into, spray-painted with graffiti, or burned down.

Turning the corner onto Pacific Highway, John could see his precious building, with the big "Der Wienerschnitzel" sign, standing just as he had left it. He breathed a sigh of relief and even chuckled at himself for his obsessive thoughts. Getting into character, he put on his white paper hat with the Der Wienerschnitzel logo, tied the little red scarf around his neck, and began day one! He mixed up a starter pot of chili, which would be enough to carry him through into early afternoon if business was what he hoped it would be.

By ten o'clock, his friends and family had arrived and parked their cars in the lot as John had instructed. Remembering old advice, he wanted to give the impression to anyone driving by that the place was busy, but not so busy that a customer couldn't get in. Phil circled the drive-thru in his car while Myrna stood at the window holding Teresa's hand, pretending that she was ordering. His basketball buddy Paul Hironimus was also there, along with Marty and Glen Bell. They all came to support the opening.

When not a single customer had turned up by eleven o'clock, Glen reminded John that the first day was no indication of how well he would do. "People need time to get familiar with anything new in their neighborhood. Don't panic. A few customers will try it out, and then word of mouth will spread." By the end of the day, a handful of people had stopped by. A few actually placed orders, but most of them were "lookie-loos," just curious about the drive-thru and the menu. John graciously thanked each of them for coming and encouraged them to tell their friends. By the end of the day, it was hardly the grand opening John had envisioned, but it was a beginning.

In a few days, just as Glen Bell had predicted, the

neighborhood slowly became aware of the new hot dog stand with the crazy name. It checked off all the enticing boxes for customers: fast service, great food, cheap prices—and a unique drive-thru feature where you didn't even have to get out of the car to order. Within a few weeks, the store was breaking even, and within a few months, it was actually turning a small profit. That was good news, but John wasn't content just yet. He yearned to hear the steady *cha-ching* of the cash register and knew he needed that something extra to set him apart from his competition. He needed that X factor.

Directly across from John's stand was a small real estate office owned by a man named Robert Trujillo. Bob, as his friends called him, had worked with Glen Bell on acquiring properties for his taco stands. During that time, he had helped Glen with an even newer enterprise he was launching called Taco Bell. Bob had originally sold Glen the property that Der Wienerschnitzel now stood on, and he was thrilled to see the fast-food stand built on what was formerly a wasted empty lot. He and John were like-minded and struck up an immediate friendship. Bob had been president of the Wilmington Chamber of Commerce and was an honorary mayor of Wilmington, which meant that he knew a great deal about the area. This, of course, interested John.

Every day on his break, John headed over to Bob Trujillo's office to ask him a million questions: What were the hot areas for business in Wilmington? Where were his competitors planning to open new stores? What traffic patterns were most conducive to fast-food restaurants? John just seemed to know exactly what to ask. Bob worked with his best friend from elementary school, Bill Linder.

Before joining Bob in the real estate business, Bill worked as a longshoreman at the Port of Long Beach. Every day from his desk window, Bill could see John crossing the highway heading for their office. He'd call out to Bob: "Here comes that Galardi kid again." In truth, they liked John's eager and enthusiastic visits.

Bob and Bill saw that X factor within John and were both interested in how high this bright young man would rise—and how they could help him get there. After all, they were in the business of selling real estate. Down the line, John could be a good customer if his Der Wienerschnitzel idea took off.

On one of his daily excursions to Bob's office, John mentioned he wanted to add some kind of special sandwich to the menu. Bill Linder quickly recommended a local place in Santa Ana that featured a Polish sausage sandwich. Right away, John wanted to try it. He grabbed Phil, who was managing the Taco Tia stand in Long Beach, and the two of them made the forty-five-minute drive to Santa Ana. It was a funky little sandwich shop with a simple and limited menu. One of the few choices was a sandwich that was essentially a grilled Polish sausage sliced lengthwise and opened flat on rye bread with a slice of Swiss cheese, a dill pickle, and mustard. It was incredibly delicious, and most importantly, it was easy to make and fit in perfectly with the Der Wienerschnitzel concept. They decided then and there to add it to the menu at the premium price of thirty cents.

It was just what John was searching for, and it became an instant winner. Customers came back for it time and time again, and the addition created a significant uptick in business. John wondered if adding a few other specialty items would have the same effect. In his usual interrogatory manner, John asked everyone, "What's one new thing you would like to see on the menu?" Baked beans and French fries received the most votes. John thought that beans and hot dogs were a natural combination, so Der Wienerschnitzel began offering a cup of baked beans as a side dish. Surprisingly, they weren't a big seller, so he decided to give French fries a try. He took the gamble, invested in a deep fryer, and started on test batches until he found the best cooking technique to make the perfect-tasting fries. On the first day they were offered, they outsold baked beans ten to one. *Cha-ching!* Beans were out and fries were in.

With all the additions and tweaks, the stand was taking off, and John was working harder than ever. He knew there was no time to rest, since competitors were always trying to gain on each other. Taking a page out of Glen Bell's marketing playbook, John offered special promotions and passed out coupons in the neighborhood. He even honored coupons from other stores, figuring that the discount he offered would guarantee repeat business. He came up with the clever idea of having his workers grill onions, because he knew that mouth-watering smell alone could entice customers to come in. He also put up twinkling lights outside the store to catch the attention of passing drivers. The pursuit of how to get the most customers was never-ending, and it took up most of his time.

***

Needless to say, there was hardly any time for John and Myrna to be together as a couple. She had to constantly remind herself that someday, when the business was on a more solid footing, John wouldn't have to work so hard. She hoped that it would happen sooner rather than later, but after three years of marriage, Myrna saw just how big John's ambitions were. She sensed he would never be entirely satisfied with the status quo, and she was right. As soon as the first Der Wienerschnitzel turned a profit, John was already planning on opening another store. He believed that owning one store would only take you so far. It wasn't until you owned a number of stores that you could make serious money.

Whenever John and Myrna were out driving, no matter where they were headed, their trip always turned into a search for a potential new location for Der Wienerschnitzel. Myrna remembers John behind the wheel of their convertible, constantly turning to look back at an empty lot on some busy corner they had just passed or glancing at the rearview mirror. "John," she would cry out in fear, "keep your eyes on

the road! We're going to get into an accident." To John, his eyes were always on the road . . . the road to success.

***

Despite these reconnaissance missions, it was Bob Trujillo who ultimately helped John find the perfect second location in Wilmington. This time, John would buy the land outright rather than lease it. Once again, he engaged Macy Coffin to build the store on the same terms and conditions he'd offered on the first Der Wienerschnitzel. Macy was already thrilled to be receiving the monthly check for 6 percent of the gross profits, so he was more than ready to turn those profits a second time. Bob Trujillo, Bill Linder, and Macy Coffin all agreed that John was the kind of person anyone would want to get into business with. He was kind, intelligent, and levelheaded, he never lost his temper, and he had a great sense of humor. He was basically just a great guy. Perhaps his best trait was that he never saw himself as above anyone else. He'd been a janitor and a boss, so he appreciated the true value of both positions and everything in between. That is an invaluable and unique perspective to have in life—one that cannot be taught.

With the second store opening, John recognized that he would no longer be able to do everything himself. He was going to have to put together a management team that could handle a dynamic, growing business. The first place he turned to for managerial talent was his two best friends from his basketball team, of course. These were guys he trusted, not only because they were friends, but also because they shared the same core values. At the time, Ron Bryant was working for Tucson Bearing, and Paul Hironimus was still employed as a draftsman in an engineering office. When John offered them a position managing a hot dog stand, they both laughed. They'd seen the kind of life that John was leading and how tethered he was to Der Wienerschnitzel day and night, and it just wasn't the kind of life they imagined for themselves. Eventually, though, they came around to John's way of thinking.

When the second Der Wienerschnitzel opened in December 1962, the name was already locally recognized, and to John's great surprise, the location was immediately successful. Suddenly, John was making more money than he could have imagined. The notion that this little hot dog idea might grow into something big became more than just a pitch to his friends. It became his mission. Symbols of successful fast-food chains like McDonald's and KFC were everywhere along the Pacific Coast Highway and throughout Los Angeles. That was what John wanted. He wanted a visual representation of Der Wienerschnitzel that was instantly recognizable. He was ready to start creating a brand.

Through his builder, Macy, John met architect Bob McKay, who had designed the distinctive hacienda motif for Glen Bell's new Taco Bell chain. John explained to McKay that he was looking for a signature building, something that people would instantly recognize as Der Wienerschnitzel. McKay mulled it over for a few days, and when they next met, he presented John with his concept. McKay had come up with the idea of an Alpine-style A-frame chalet, which was inspired by the company's German name. John absolutely loved it and immediately envisioned how it would look, with the bright red, sloping roof topped by a yellow-and-red "Der Wienerschnitzel" sign. Magical.

And so, in 1962, the first Der Wienerschnitzel A-frame— and third location overall—opened in Compton. The unusual architecture received some great media attention, complete with pictures and articles in the local South Bay area newspapers. It was every bit as memorable and eye-catching as the Golden Arches, Colonel Sanders's smiling face, and Glen Bell's swinging purple Taco Bell. Three stores quickly turned to four, and John needed help running them. He pressed Phil and their parents into helping out, as well as his cousin, Phil Pisciotta. His basketball buddies were still hanging on the sidelines, but they kept up with what was going on with Der Wienerschnitzel and were amazed at what John had accomplished in such a short period of time.

It wasn't just the buying and building of the new stores that was occupying John's mind. He was still constantly working on how to make the menu items tastier and the stores more cost-effective. For example, John insisted that the hot dog buns be perfectly steamed, warm and soft. Not every commercially produced bun could stand up to the steaming process and hold together, though, so John found a local bakery run by a man named Andy Soltis. He made hot dog buns exactly the way John liked them. John liked them so much, in fact, that he bought the bakery and had Andy work exclusively for Der Wienerschnitzel.

With that acquisition, John was building a vertically integrated business.

***

On the operational level, John was a real stickler about what he referred to as "running orders." John had devised a system for speeding up the drive-thru ordering process. When a car drove in, before it even got to the order window, John would have one of the servers stationed outside to greet the driver and take the order. The server would then run inside and repeat the order to the cook at the grill. By the time the car pulled up to the window, their order would be ready to go. The "runner-chargers," as John called them, were one of the personal services that made Der Wienerschnitzel unique. John had a phenomenal memory, and for him, it was easy to remember every detail of every order, which was not the case for the majority of the servers. But John was adamant that writing the orders down on a piece of paper was a waste of time: "Get it in your head, and keep it there until you give it to the cook. Then get back out there and take the next order. You'll get the hang of it." That was John's edict, and everyone followed it. With practice, the runner-chargers all became quite capable of remembering long lists of detailed orders. It was a skill that would diminish when business became hectic, and the runner-chargers jotted crib notes on cup lids or paper bags. The system was eventually jettisoned when the highly efficient system of speakerphone ordering was introduced industry-wide in the 1970s.

By 1963, Bob Trujillo and Bill Linder began focusing on finding locations outside the local area for the Der Wienerschnitzel brand. John respected their suggestions, but he always had to make a personal assessment of the site before he made a decision. His instincts had guided him correctly up until that point, and he wasn't about to abandon the tactic that had led him so far. His attention to detail was great for business, but it didn't have the same effect on his family.

Every time he drove to a potential site, it was time away from them. As the days and months went by, he realized that he was spending less and less time with Myrna and his daughters, Teresa and baby Karen, but there was no relief in sight in the short run, so long as he wanted to stay on the fast track to success.

For the first time in his life, John had enough money to do whatever he wanted. It was a stark contrast to his upbringing, but more than anything, he wanted to give his family what he never had. His vision of happiness included a nicer house and an even bigger bank account that would make him feel safe and secure in terms of his family's well-being. Myrna was also raised in a family that was used to doing without, but a simple life was all she required to be happy.

She and John were opposites in that way, so when John walked in the door of their little two-bedroom bungalow in Wilmington and announced, "I just bought us a house in Rolling Hills," she was taken aback. Once again, John had made a major life decision that Myrna was expected to go along with.

As levelheaded as John was about business, when it came to spending personal money, he had a bit of a flamboyant streak. Established in 1936, Rolling Hills was a wealthy residential development on the Palos Verdes Peninsula with two-to-ten-acre home lots. Known for its equestrian lifestyle and bucolic setting, Rolling Hills had miles of horse trails, vast open spaces, and a spectacular view of the Pacific Ocean below. In the years since the developers first broke ground, Rolling Hills had achieved a reputation as one of the finest neighborhoods in Southern California. It was also where Marty and Glen Bell had bought their house a few years before.

Architect Bob McKay's rendering of the A-frame design.

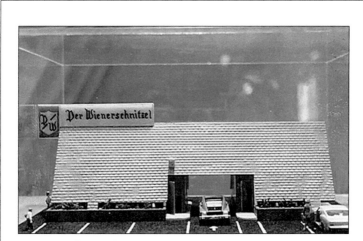

Three-dimensional model featuring the drive-thru.

A League of His Own

3

By 1964, John, Myrna, and their daughters were living the California Dream. Cozy in his idyllic dream house, John had an easy commute from the Palos Verdes Peninsula to the four Der Wienerschnitzel stores he now owned. There were also, of course, more stores on the drawing board.

Though John recognized he was a good leader, he knew he lacked a solid business background. Other than taking cues from his mentor, Glen Bell, he understood that he had a lot to learn if he was going to grow Der Wienerschnitzel from a mom-and-pop operation into a corporate juggernaut. He had some hard learning to do and knew that getting advice from coworkers wasn't going to cut it anymore. He decided to hit the books and study experts in the business field.

A Claremont College professor of business management

named Peter Drucker greatly appealed to John. He religiously read Drucker's books and felt they provided John with a template to follow as he built his company. Throughout his business career, John would refer to Drucker's books as a source of guidance, and he often quoted Drucker to his management team and franchisees. John could easily articulate the answers to some of Drucker's questions. The answer to, "What is our mission?" was self-evident: to serve high-quality fast food at competitive prices in an efficient manner. "Who is our customer?" took a bit more thought. It was easy just to say, "Anyone who's hungry," but there wasn't much insight to be gained from that answer. As John mulled this over, he realized that the answer to this question would drive every decision he made regarding the future growth and branding of Der Wienerschnitzel.

In order to define his customer base, he began by quizzing everyone who had hands-on experience in the Der Wienerschnitzel family. He turned to his store managers, the runner-chargers who took the orders, and the employees who worked the order windows. He wanted specific information about his customers. Who was buying in the early morning? What time did people show up after the workday closed? Who brought their children? What percentage of older people did they attract? Were teenagers driving through or just walking up? How much was the average ticket per customer? What were they buying? And on and on.

John wasn't shy about interviewing his customers directly,

either, in order to answer Drucker's third question, "What does the customer value?" Customers were quick to offer opinions regarding the menu, service, and pricing, such as how much chili to put on a hot dog, what new soft drink to add, or what kind of family specials they would like to see on the menu. At neighborhood barbecues, family gatherings, and basketball games, John couldn't restrain himself from asking guests what they thought of Der Wienerschnitzel. He was perpetually in work mode. Usually, one of his buddies would have to remind him to relax. Over the years, he turned even family meals into focus groups. As his older daughter, Teresa, remembers, "Dad loved to grill me and Karen on what we would eat or drink if we had a dollar. I remember him asking us, 'What would you buy or how far would you drive if you had a dollar and a car and only thirty-five minutes for lunch?'"

John kept meticulous records of the daily sales at each store and the cost of labor, food, supplies, and overhead. He had an uncanny memory for numbers and could tell you within a dollar what each store was generating on a daily basis and the average ticket per customer. By the time the fourth store opened in 1963, he could hear the *cha-ching* of the cash register loud and clear, which had been his goal from the very beginning. His consolidated financials indicated that Der Wienerschnitzel was showing a healthy profit across the board.

But John was also facing a dilemma if he wanted to keep

growing the company. He knew the *strength* of his organization came from his personal dedication and his involvement in the day-to-day operations, but paradoxically, that was also Der Wienerschnitzel's weakness. He could not expand beyond what he could accomplish himself. If growth was his main goal, he needed to figure out a way to incentivize others and make them part of the solution. John decided it was time to franchise.

John knew that Glen Bell had recently adopted franchising as a method to attract individuals and their capital to grow Taco Bell. There were many variables to the concept of franchising. Basically, the oversight of the franchise business was left to the Federal Trade Commission rather than the Securities and Exchange Commission. This meant that franchising was not strictly viewed as an investment, although franchising was a way of attracting other people's money.

The basic feature of franchising was that the franchisee paid an initial buy-in fee to the parent company and a monthly 5 percent of sales for the use of the name, the brand identity, and the support of the parent company.

Each franchisee was required to purchase their own equipment and supplies (typically from the parent company) and was responsible for hiring and supervising local staff. Most importantly, a franchisee was required to uphold the operating standards of the parent company and adhere to the basic menu. In turn, the parent company provided training and support for managers and workers.

They also paid the rental fee to the owner of the land on which the restaurant was built, as well as advertising costs.

Franchise agreements were typically written for a period of ten to fifteen years. At the end of the agreement, both parties had to agree to extend the term of the franchise agreement. At that time, the franchisee was often required to make additional investments in their individual stores, such as upgrading equipment. Convinced that the franchise model was the key to Der Wienerschnitzel's growth and the way to bring in investors and partners, John incorporated Der Wienerschnitzel in the state of California in 1964. He then hired an attorney to handle all the paperwork and draft a franchise agreement. At the same time, he put together a management team that would help engineer the growth of the company.

His first direct corporate hire was Bob Trujillo as director of real estate and investments. It would be up to Bob to attract partners willing to invest in the company in order to build a number of stores before lining up franchisees. The company also needed working capital to function until franchisee royalty fees and other payments started rolling in. Raising capital was a new venture for Bob Trujillo, but he felt confident. Bob's many business contacts, coupled with John's persuasive personality and exciting vision for Der Wienerschnitzel, would help to pull it all off. Admittedly, he and John were two brash, young entrepreneurs who were both learning on the job. "Fake it till you make it" comes to mind.

Construction of the buildings was paid for by the landowner, a group of investors, or Der Wienerschnitzel. John was open to making any kind of deal that would result in opening another store. Phil later said, "It was the Wild West, and everyone was shooting from the hip." During the company's infancy, everyone operated according to the principle "do whatever works." Bob obviously believed in John and felt that Der Wienerschnitzel had tremendous upside potential. He was a convincing fundraiser and succeeded in attracting investments from people in his business network who trusted him and were willing to get in on the ground floor. It also didn't hurt that the hot dogs were delicious and the stores were unmistakable on busy street corners.

With money in the bank, Bob and Bill Linder were tasked with finding vacant lots for new stores. They searched in Long Beach, Carson, Torrance, and San Pedro. The real estate was cheap, and the customer base was similar to that of the four operating Der Wienerschnitzel stores. The two men identified a number of sites that met John's criteria. Once John had looked over the property and given his approval, Bob negotiated the price and closed the deal. In short order, Bob secured the necessary building permits, and five more stores were under construction by 1964.

While sitting in a favorite cafeteria in Long Beach with Macy, going over the construction details for the new A-frames, John scribbled a note to himself: *Contact Ron re. Tucson.* John was already envisioning expanding Der Wienerschnitzel throughout the southwestern United States. He landed on Tucson, Arizona, as a launching pad, because it was an ideal market. It had loads of cars, commuters, and planned communities with high-density housing. The year-round sunshine was an added bonus. And best of all, it was the new home of Ron "Ronnie" Bryant, one of John's best friends and his teammate on the Dominguez Water Company basketball team. Over the years, he and his wife, Jeanne, had become very close friends with John and Myrna. Teresa, Karen, and the Bryants' four daughters were all around the same age, so the two families often vacationed together. Ron had recently been relocated from Long Beach to Tucson.

More than once, John made Ron an offer to come work for him, but each time, Ron turned him down. Ron was very happy with his position at the bearing company; he was making a good salary and had a comfortable life. He told John, "Why would I walk away from a steady salary and take a gamble on Der Wienerschnitzel? You're my good buddy, but I think I'll stick to ball bearings." But now, as John mulled over the plans for the next five stores, he had the numbers to show Ron exactly how much money he could make in the fast-food industry. Ron was so impressed that he agreed to talk it over with his wife.

Jeanne then talked it over with Myrna. Myrna talked it over with John. After a lot of soul searching and skillful salesmanship, John assured Ron that he would stand behind

him until he got his feet under him financially.

***

In 1966, Ron Bryant became the first out-of-state franchisee for Der Wienerschnitzel. John couldn't have been happier. This was, after all, always how he imagined his dreams for the company would come to fruition. He wanted people he knew and trusted to be a part of its success. His success would be their success. The Bryants started with one store in Tucson and a $9,000 loan from John to cover the opening costs. They agreed to pay off the loan in one year. It turned out that the profits were so good that, within three months, the Bryants were able to pay John back. Within one year, they opened four more stores in Arizona. It was incredible.

By 1965, it seemed as if John and Der Wienerschnitzel were an entrepreneur's dream. Everyone who had bought into the business was turning a profit, and the returns on investment exceeded all expectations. In the 1960s, the United States experienced its longest uninterrupted period of economic expansion in its history. By 1965, General Motors, Standard Oil, and the Ford Motor Company had larger incomes than all the farms in the US. For the first two years of the Johnson administration, the inflation rate was under 2 percent. The urbanization of America and the economic boom definitely contributed to Der Wienerschnitzel's success. How long all of it would continue was anyone's guess—it's hard to predict a bubble bursting. It was a great time nonetheless.

Ron Bryant was so excited about how things were panning out for him and Jeanne that he contacted another old basketball teammate, Paul Hironimus, and said, "Paul, you've got to get in on this. Call John immediately." It took some convincing on Ron's part, since Paul had a predictable, solid career as a draftsman in an engineering firm and a family to support. But Paul was finally convinced and called John. "Is that offer of work at Der Wienerschnitzel still good?" he asked. Another buddy joining the team made John ecstatic. It was all coming together. With his background in engineering, Paul could bring many worthwhile skills to the company. That said, John didn't want him to just manage a store; he wanted Paul to analyze the business from the ground up. He started him in the kitchen, slapping mustard on hot dogs and running orders.

After three days on the job, Paul looked in the mirror and thought, "Is this what I gave up my well-paying job in an air-conditioned office for? So that I could run after cars in a mustard-stained shirt wearing a funny little yellow hat? I must be crazy." But John knew exactly what he was doing. His decision to put Paul in an entry-level position was sheer genius. In short order, Paul identified ways to improve the operations of Der Wienerschnitzel. After only a few weeks of sweating it out in the kitchen behind the grill, Paul noticed how the hot dog buns were steamed in a separate piece of equipment that required constant maintenance. To address the problem, Paul designed an ingenious system that allowed the steam that was already being generated from cooking the hot dogs to be diverted into a chamber to steam the buns. It was so successful and cost-effective that the equipment was introduced in all existing stores and became part of the standard equipment package for all future Der Wienerschnitzels. His idea was a huge win for all.

As the champagne popped and confetti flew, the new year rolled in. It was a great start to 1966: almost all twenty Der Wienerschnitzel stores in Southern California and Arizona were reporting healthy profits. John's entire family was now involved in managing or owning individual stores, including his parents and his cousin Phil. Based on the strength of the company's balance sheet and pro forma income statement, Bob Trujillo was able to attract numerous investors, including some Texas oil millionaires. He even convinced his sister, Esther Beard, and her husband to become franchisees with a stand in San Pedro. As many early franchisees and investors pointed out, it wasn't just the financials that made the company so attractive, it was also John. His trustworthiness, self-confidence, and charm were at their peak and continued to win people over as they always had. John was a rainmaker of sorts. People believed in him and were willing to follow wherever he was headed.

As Der Wienerschnitzel moved into other western states, everyone in the company had to make sure they were on point. They had to maintain control of the franchisees and be confident that the stores could compete effectively in new markets. The huge constant that always helped Der Wienerschnitzel was that no one else was serving hot dogs in a big way. That alone gave Der Wienerschnitzel a competitive advantage over other fast-food chains and made it an attractive option for potential franchisees. In addition, the buy-in price of $20,000 was less than what McDonald's and some of the other chains were charging. This meant that those with less credit or savings could still find a way into the fast-food industry.

John was on fire with his plans for expansion. This time his gut told him that San Bernardino was fertile territory for the Der Wienerschnitzel brand. He took a trip there to scope out the scene and ended up at a real estate office called the Royal Huntley. When he entered, he came upon twenty-six-year-old Kirk Robison sitting behind a desk. He was a newbie who had just started working in real estate. For Kirk, that day was one which he would never forget. "So this guy named John Galardi had seen a sign on a property with Royal Huntley's name on it. He walked into the office and I happened to be there. He introduced himself and said, 'I've got a few hot dog stands called Wienerschnitzel, and I'm looking to open some new locations in San Bernardino.' And that quick hello was the start of our relationship."

John found Kirk Robison to be as much of a go-getter as he was. John seemed to have a way of attracting people similarly minded to him. Kirk scouted out prime locations for Der Wienerschnitzel stores and helped John successfully deal with local landowners and builders. "A year later, John called me and asked if I would be interested in taking over the job of finding new locations for Wienerschnitzel in all of Southern California. I wasn't committed to living in San Bernardino, and it was easy enough for me to relocate, so I said, 'Sure, let's talk about it.' We met at a coffee shop in West Covina. 'Here's the deal. If you come to work for me, I'll pay you one hundred and fifty dollars a week, and I'll give you a Texaco credit card to pay for your gas.' That was more than I was making in real estate, so I agreed, and John hired me on the spot." And just like that, Kirk Robison was in on the ground floor of the great fast-food expansion.

On John's twenty-eighth birthday, he realized he had exceeded his initial goals for the company, but he was still formulating ways to drive the growth of Der Wienerschnitzel even further. Whether he had heard this quotation from one of his mentors is unclear, but his actions certainly reflected Michelangelo's philosophy: "The great danger for most of us lies not in setting our aim too high and falling short, but in setting our aim too low, and achieving our mark."

By December 1966, there were ninety-three franchised and company-owned Der Wienerschnitzel stores in Southern California, Texas, Illinois, Arizona, and Georgia. Over the next year, the company created subsidiaries to service the stores. Der Wienerschnitzel already owned the Swedish Bakery, which manufactured bread products for the chain. They also owned an equipment company that purchased kitchen equipment that it then leased to the franchisees. In a five-month period in 1967, Kirk Robison and his team closed an incredible thirty-eight deals in eleven states. With the large number of additions, John's attorneys suggested that he consolidate his various enterprises, which were originally structured as sole proprietorships, into an umbrella corporation. Der Wienerschnitzel Unlimited, the name of the corporation, started issuing stock to John and his investors.

By the end of 1967, despite the size and scale of Der Wienerschnitzel Unlimited, it still remained in line with John's vision. It was still first and foremost a family-owned business, which John was pretty proud of. People often wonder what it was about John Galardi that set him soaring at such a young age or how he became such a visionary. Some credit his laser-like focus on business, or his burning desire to escape the poverty of his childhood, but those qualities can be compared to many others who tried and failed. What John had was a deep sense of kindness and a respect for all people. That sentiment seems simple enough, but those attributes are a hard find in the cutthroat business world. In that often-angst-ridden environment, John somehow never lost his temper or his sense of humor, and he never lost touch with the better angels of his nature.

He stayed on his moral track, and that propelled him into a league all his own.

The iconic red roof A-frame Der Wienerschnitzel.

The first Der Wienerschnitzel store, Wilmington, California, 1961.
The start of something big.

Quid Pro Quo

4

As the permissiveness of the sixties rolled toward a new decade, images played out in the media showing the younger generation expressing love and understanding. At the same time, tens of thousands of people protested the Vietnam War and injustice through marches and riots that sometimes turned deadly. Ordinary Americans tried to make sense of all of this while getting on with their lives. The soundtrack of this era was best captured by the Beatles in "Revolution" and the musical *Hair*. Pop artist Andy Warhol raised mundane Campbell's soup cans and pictures of Chairman Mao to the level of high art.

By October 1967, a paranoid President Johnson instructed the FBI and CIA to investigate anti-Vietnam War protesters. His administration suspected Communists were responsible.

The economy, while still robust, was showing signs of inflationary pressure, and the prime rate (the interest charged to corporate America) was hovering just above 6 percent, with predictions that it might increase. Uncertainty reigned, and for many Americans, it was a confusing time.

John Galardi was steeped in his own daily dramas thanks to the rapid expansion of his business. Some of the early Der Wienerschnitzel stores, owned by partnerships made up of business associates Bob Trujillo had put together, were beginning to show signs of trouble from the strain of being spread too thin. Bob recalls, "You know it's all blue sky. You're going in wide open thinking you're going to make a fortune. You're looking at McDonald's out there building like crazy, and you think, 'We can do the same thing.' John was super good as far as optimism was concerned, and working with him was always great, but neither of us had a solid business background, so we just learned from doing it the hard way. Some of those first stores had to be closed down because they weren't profitable, and some of our friends lost money. But what we learned from that was the hot dog concept is difficult. It's not like tacos or chicken. It's a snack and it's lunch only. It's harder to make it successful, and we hadn't yet found the formula to make it work, but we knew we would because John never stopped trying—he would never give up."

John and Bob sat down at one of their regular brainstorming sessions to mull over what was happening company wide. Kirk was now in Texas opening up new territories for Der

Wienerschnitzel. He was also slated to go to Chicago to develop stores in the Midwest. Big money was coming in from the royalty fees and property rentals paid by franchisees and from purchases of supplies, equipment, and produce. But the rapid expansion already underway was quickly eating up all their capital. The two men were in agreement that some new creative idea was needed to generate additional working capital to pay for the current and future commitments they'd already made. John had an interesting offer from his attorney Richard "Dick" Hodge that he wanted to run by Bob.

Hodge had been handling John's legal affairs for the past couple of years, and the two men had become close friends. Hodge was a sophisticated Beverly Hills lawyer who greatly admired John's intelligence and ambition. He could see beyond John's Missouri farm boy persona and knew that he was smarter than everyone else in the room. Richard and John enjoyed regular drinks together at the Luau restaurant or other swanky Beverly Hills bars, surrounded by glamorous movie stars and sophisticated businesspeople. John thought that by associating himself with Dick Hodge, some of that sophistication would rub off. He respected Dick, so when he had something to say, John listened intently.

Hodge planned to arrange a $1 million loan with the John Hancock Mutual Life Insurance Company in Boston, which would be enough to cover Der Wienerschnitzel's short- and medium-term cash needs, until the stores coming online started generating sufficient revenue to pay back the loan over time. Both John and Bob could see that the Hancock option was risky—they would be taking on enormous debt. Up to this point in the company's history, they'd been funding all their needs from cash flow. But with the franchise concept firmly in place and new franchisee inquiries and interest pouring in daily to the home office in Torrance, this seemed like a viable deal.

John grabbed a pen and a napkin and started crunching the numbers. Every new franchise would immediately bring in $20,000 in cash up front, which, in addition to the 5 percent royalty generated by new stores, would enable Der Wienerschnitzel to service the debt. There would obviously be costs associated with the building and opening of new stores, but the accumulation of that regular cash in the bank would pull the company out of a cash crunch and (hopefully) fuel robust growth.

This was music to John Galardi's ears—a step up into the big leagues. He'd been paying close attention to Glen Bell's franchise success with Taco Bell and witnessed McDonald's popping up on every street corner. Ray Kroc, the president of McDonald's, at one point even contacted John to talk about a possible deal with Der Wienerschnitzel, but other than a sit-down meeting, the conversation never went anywhere. John never wavered from his ambition to "be as big as Taco Bell, maybe even as big as McDonald's, someday." He remembered a Mark Twain line that had stuck with him from his college days: "Twenty years from now you will be more disappointed by the things that you didn't do than by the ones you did do."

John pushed the paper napkin toward Bob. "Let's do it."

Dick Hodge set up the meeting with John and the executives at John Hancock. Their credit department had done due diligence on the financial statements prepared by Der Wienerschnitzel's accountants. The numbers looked pretty good, but more importantly, the execs were very impressed with John Galardi.

They quickly agreed to commit to a $1 million loan. John was relieved that Hancock didn't require him to personally sign the loan; this was a corporate loan, and if things went south, John's personal assets were protected as well as his other business ventures, which were kept apart from Der Wienerschnitzel Unlimited thanks to his team of lawyers.

But there was a quid pro quo. John had to agree to purchase thirty building sites Hancock had foreclosed on that were sitting in their real estate portfolio and not producing any revenue. John Galardi and John Hancock were definitely in business together. John got the money he needed, and Hancock unloaded their nonperforming real estate. In addition, Hancock received 10 percent of the company shares.

Once the Hancock deal closed and the check for $1 million was deposited in the corporate bank account, John felt a new lease on life. He set himself a goal to open at least two hundred more stores by 1970, and to help him realize that dream, he promoted Bob Trujillo from director of real estate and investments to vice president of Der Wienerschnitzel.

The expansion program kicked into high gear, and red-roofed A-frames began dotting the American landscape from California to Florida. In less than seven years, Der Wienerschnitzel grew from a local enterprise to a national chain, and there was no end in sight.

But why stop at hot dogs? Why not start another new food franchise? What about fish-and-chips? When John Galardi had an idea, he went with it. Within four months of receiving the $1 million loan from Hancock, John had opened his second franchise business, Friar Fish, with the first four fish restaurants opening in California. They were slow to get started, but John had been through that before. The fish chain was already finding franchisee interest in Hawaii, Nevada, Oregon, and Washington, DC, so John was looking to have another winner on his hands.

During this time, John's main focus was on the marketing side of Der Wienerschnitzel. The company needed to help all their new franchisees attract customers and make money for themselves and the company. Advertising was a major factor in the fast-food industry, where even loyal customers could be very fickle. Household names had to constantly find new and exciting ways to stay competitive and deliver their message through clever and catchy print, radio, and television advertising. Memorable characters and catchy phrases were a must for grabbing a customer's attention. *"Der fixin's are derlightful, der's fun in every biteful"* became Der Wienerschnitzel's first advertising slogan in 1967. To add to "der fun," there was a radio jingle that went like this:

Der Wienerschnitzel, Wienerschnitzel,
This must be the place.
Just drive right in
and put a great big hot dog in your face.

John's daughter Teresa fondly recalls, "I would hear classmates humming that song in the hallways at school, and sometimes people would see me and start singing that song on purpose." That clever ditty was the work of Robert and Richard Sherman, two young songwriters, whose famed songwriting career for Walt Disney (*It's a Small World, Mary Poppins, Chitty Chitty Bang Bang, The Jungle Book*) would go on to earn multiple Academy Awards. It was an early sign that John Galardi knew how to spot the best.

And the first thirty-second TV spot had this snappy jingle:

Fun, Der Wienerschnitzel
Yum, Der Wienerschnitzel
Come to Der Wienerschnitzel, fun yum yum
Eat at Der Wienerschnitzel, treat at Der Wienerschnitzel
Wienerschnitzel hot dogs are der top dogs
Yum yummy yummy yum, every bite is full of fun
Bring your dad and mummy
You would be so happy if you come, yum yum
Der fixin's are derlightful

Der's fun in every biteful
At der happy Wienerschnitzel, yum yum hot dog

There was no doubt John was taking a page out of Glen Bell's playbook. He might not have always had klieg lights or live entertainment, but he enlisted the help of pretty girls, cavalcades of cars lining up in front of stores, the ever-useful coupons that promoted opening-day specials, and of course advertising, advertising, and more advertising.

Myrna recalls that in the local fast-food community, they all attended each other's opening days. Even though they were rivals for the same fast-food dollars, on a personal level, they were all friends. Standing around sipping a soda or munching on a hot dog to make the place look busy was how they showed their support for each other. And in the late 1960s, there were a lot of openings to attend. It seemed as if every week, two or three Der Wienerschnitzel stores were breaking ground.

One of the major differences between Der Wienerschnitzel and most other fast-food chains was that Der Wienerschnitzel was still a family-owned company, completely under the control of John Galardi. By comparison, McDonald's went public in 1965, and that same year, Colonel Harland David Sanders sold a majority interest in KFC to financier Jack C. Massey. It was reported that Colonel Sanders just didn't like the business side of the business.

Seeing all the economic changes in the fast-food industry

and the equally dramatic shifts in Der Wienerschnitzel's business, John was forced to think about taking the company public. Pressure to grow the business combined with the commitment to repay the Hancock loan made this a serious option. But the idea of being subject to Securities and Exchange Commission (SEC) regulations and a board of directors wasn't something that sat well with John's independent mindset. On the other hand, a public offering of stock would infuse the company with enough cash to cover all their loan costs and fund ongoing construction and land purchases. Within his circle of advisers, John found a lot of support for the idea. Richard Hodge notes, "The first high point [in the company's history] was when we secured the financing from John Hancock, and the second was John's decision to go out with a public stock offering."

In the September 18, 1968, issue of *California Business*, an interview with John Galardi was published with the headline "Name of the Game Is Money." His interview revealed an abundance of self-confidence and optimism about a proposed stock offering of 150,000 shares at ten dollars a share that would increase his personal wealth from $2 million to $15 million. "We're opening a hundred new units a year, or about two a week. We might raise that to two hundred a year," John said. The reporter added, "There should be five hundred of Galardi's colorful hot dog stands around the country by 1971." Most risk-taking entrepreneurs like John had an unshakable faith in their own story, and John was acting accordingly. The underwriters felt fairly certain that the initial public offering would be successful.

A notification of the stock offering for 500,000 shares, at a reduced price of five dollars per share, was filed in February 1969. The purposes of the stock sale included acquisition of land and construction of Der Wienerschnitzel stands, site acquisition of some thirty Friar Fish stores in Washington, DC, and an increase in the company's working capital. It was a great idea at the right time.

In May of that same year, Glen Bell also filed a registration statement with the SEC for a public offering of 250,000 shares of Taco Bell stock at fourteen dollars per share in order to repay his short-term bank debt and provide the company with working capital. In addition, the anticipated sale would fund the purchase price of seven Taco Bell restaurants the company had recently acquired from franchisees.

Was this a coincidence? Probably not. It's likely John and Glen Bell were in close communication with one another, comparing notes about the structure and potential outcome of their deals. But while Glen Bell's deal was handled by a large Los Angeles-based investment banking firm, Bateman Eichler, Hill Richards Inc., John's deal was being orchestrated by a small Boston-based firm, Sterman & Gowell, Inc.

The sale of a public offering involved months of legal and financial preparations, but the impact of what it could mean for the Der Wienerschnitzel brand had everyone in the company excited.

As Der Wienerschnitzel continued to expand, with close to two hundred stores, John could no longer maintain the strict control he exercised when they were a mom-and-pop organization. Some franchisees didn't have the managerial skills to make their stands profitable, no matter how much help they were receiving from the parent company by way of marketing, personnel training, and cost controls. John was forced once again to make the tough decision to close down some locations, just as he'd done in previous years when he had to shutter some of the stores owned by early investor friends of Bob Trujillo's. John knew that survival of the fittest was par for the course in big franchises; he'd seen Glen Bell close down stores that weren't performing up to company standards.

These were tough decisions, but done for the greater good of the company. John did his best to pay the franchisees back their initial investment, but inevitably, some franchisees whose entire life savings were tied up in the business suffered severe financial losses. Conversely, there were stores like Ron Bryant's in Arizona and Esther Beard's in San Pedro and Hemet that were doing really great business.

Esther was Bob Trujillo's sister and one of the earliest franchisees in California. She'd had a longtime job at an insurance agency, and her husband had worked for Atlantic Richfield. They both gave up well-paying jobs to take a chance with Der Wienerschnitzel, and for them, it paid off big time. Esther describes her secret to success: "You work all the time.

You don't just take off when you want. Running a store is hard to do. I try to tell people who think they can get into a business and have somebody run it for them that it doesn't work that way. My drive-thru didn't have enough space for all the cars coming through, so I was crazy enough to take an order out on the street because I didn't want to lose the customer. I'd be taking the orders outside, and one time this kid went home and said to his mother, 'Wienerschnitzel is hiring old people now.' She replied, 'No, they're not.' He insisted, 'Yes, there's an older lady out there taking orders from the cars,' and she said, 'No, that's Mrs. Beard; she owns the place! Nobody that didn't own the business would work that hard.' So, it was hard, but you can make it if you don't mind working. We were always taught by our parents that you had to work for everything you wanted. People think you just get it without working hard, but you can't."

By the end of 1968, the company had a total of 218 stands and reported gross revenue of $14,655,000. The nonperforming stands had been jettisoned, and the company's overall balance sheet—despite the $1 million in debt on the books—looked healthy and seemed positioned to meet the stringent requirements of a public offering.

By the time the forty-page prospectus was printed and dated June 17, 1969, underwriters had started to circle the number of shares of stock that they would be responsible for selling to the public. The offering asked a price of five dollars per share for a total of 500,000 shares, or $2.5 million in proceeds. As with most IPOs, it was hoped the stock would sell for more than the initial offering price, which, over many months of legal wheeling and dealing by expensive lawyers and accountants, had been adjusted downward from the initial price of ten dollars a share.

To John and everyone involved with the deal, it seemed like clear sailing for Der Wienerschnitzel. Now all they needed was for the SEC to bless the deal, and the underwriters could take the offering to market.

A John Hancock executive hands John a check for $1 million.

Hard Times

5

The excitement of going public probably glossed over the truth that this wasn't just an effort to grow the company. In the opinion of many insiders, it was, in fact, an effort to save the company. The rapid expansion had taken a toll on the finances of Der Wienerschnitzel, and the anticipated returns had not materialized. Because the company was spending so much money opening stores, the accumulated debt was $2 million and growing at the rate of $60,000 per month. They were bleeding cash, ready to topple as the pedestal soared higher and higher. While everyone waited for the good news, John, attorney Dick Hodge, and Vice President Bob Trujillo were all keenly aware of how much was riding on the stock offering.

Bob Trujillo took the call at lunchtime. He knew

immediately from the sound of John's voice that the news wasn't good. In a measured way, John explained that the accounting firm—whose job it was to certify that the company's financial reporting was in line with SEC regulations—refused to give their blessings to the company's balance sheet, income statement, and pro forma financials, all of which were necessary for an SEC filing.

Bob's heart sank. He knew John must have been devastated. This was going to take some time to sink in, and neither he nor John could quite get their heads around this sudden reversal of fortune. The best explanation for what happened was that the company was too highly leveraged, and Der Wienerschnitzel's ability to repay its existing debt was called into question. Also, the numbers didn't adequately take into account the rise in cost of raw product: flour, meat, etc. But whatever the reason, the bottom line was that without certification, there could be no public offering.

"Jeez, John, what are we gonna do?" was all Bob could ask. In that rare moment, John didn't have an answer. Both men knew that without the capital to service the John Hancock debt, they were going to have to run very hard just to keep standing still. With over two hundred stores open and more launching every day, the money they'd received from new franchisees was already being spent daily just to keep up with the rapid pace of construction. For the first time, John was overpowered by the thought of bankruptcy. There was now a real possibility they could lose everything, and Der Wienerschnitzel would go out of business.

Bankruptcy: "utter failure or impoverishment." The very definition of the word made John's skin crawl. This wasn't just about money. This was about family, and being able to take care of them and all those who were counting on him. He knew what it meant to be financially impoverished. Escaping that demon had been the driving force of his life. Now here it was again, threatening to take away everything he'd worked so hard for. This was a fear so deeply ingrained, he was loath to face it with anyone—not his wife, not Bob Trujillo, not Richard Hodge. And in reality, maybe not even himself.

It's been said that the smarter you are, the better a trap you build for yourself.

John had become a master of keeping his thoughts and feelings under control, and now, as his world appeared on the verge of collapse, he continued to put on a brave face. Richard Hodge remembers John's reaction to the aborted public offering: "Through it all, John remained cool and calm; he knew the importance of putting on a game face. It was a brave display of courage from a thirty-one-year-old facing a major business setback that could unravel into a full-on bankruptcy." Meanwhile, in contrast to Der Wienerschnitzel's disappointment, the Taco Bell offering was successful, and by January 1970, all the stock had been sold.

One of John's great gifts was his belief that life isn't about how you get knocked down; it's all about how you get back up. John was determined to find a way to recover from this situation. He didn't have a solution, but he knew he would do it. He had to. He made a promise to himself that he would pay back every penny owed. But it was the immediate future he was most concerned about. John was aware that the news about the failure of the public offering would be a blow to everyone on the corporate side of Der Wienerschnitzel. He didn't want that panic to create chaos among the individual franchisees, so for now, it would be business as usual, both at work and at home.

It's not surprising when Myrna speaks of that time that there is a sense she was only vaguely aware of the stressful time John was going through. "Of course, there were unhappy times when things didn't go quite the way John wanted. We went through some ups and downs when the company tried to go public. And I don't know the details of that and why it didn't work, and there were a lot of expenses with New York attorneys to deal with. It was pretty much a disaster, although it did make the company remain a family business. But those were hard times."

A family business—that was a concept that John could wrap his head around.

In fact, the one regret he always had about the prospect of taking the company public was that he'd be giving up that satisfying feeling of owning a family business. As a man who always wanted to be in control of his fortune, the public offering meant that he would have to relinquish a great deal of the decision-making to a board of directors and stockholders. Der Wienerschnitzel would no longer be a nimble company able to respond quickly to his creative input. All important decisions would be made by faceless executives in boardrooms with reams of legal documents, instead of in coffee shops with stacks of paper napkins.

So if there was lemonade to be made out of these lemons, this was it. The company would remain a family-owned business, and over time, that would become the big difference between Der Wienerschnitzel and most of the other fast-food franchises swallowed up by Wall Street. Der Wienerschnitzel and all its employees would say the one thing John cherished most in life: family.

Initially, the only way John could think to pull himself out of debt was to redouble his efforts to turn a profit. He knew that it took money to make money, and whatever the company could afford was spent on advertising and branding efforts. The new company slogan was "Look for Der Red Roof." It may not have been the most creative example of advertising copy, but it certainly drove home a visual message. Additionally, flyers were an inexpensive way to capture customers, so there were all kinds of flyers tailored specifically to appeal to local clientele. There were also bold outdoor billboards, and even a few eye-catching models. The additional expense of advertising was passed on to the franchisees, and as their expenses mounted, the price of the hot dogs increased from fifteen to eighteen cents. This was a time when every penny counted.

While John continued to put on a brave face, inside the company, the cracks were beginning to widen as revenue continued to fall behind expenses. Bob Trujillo's memory of that time is painfully clear: "We built two hundred stores in three years. The volume wasn't there, and we really started losing a lot of money. We were getting a little ahead of ourselves. We owed all the vendors, we couldn't pay them, and then we had that loan with John Hancock, a million dollars or more, we couldn't pay them.

"We had a guy named Volker Brandlemeier in accounting, a German guy with a thick accent, and he would run through the hall saying, 'Vee are brrroke. Vee are super brrroke.' Those were tough times. There was never any exaggeration of what we were doing or trying to do. It's hard when people trust you, and you're honest with them, and then things go wrong."

Bob and John were using every trick in the book to cut corners, including making some painful decisions about the franchisees. Desperate times called for desperate measures, and when they finally realized they could no longer shield the individual owners from the truth, they had to be open about the state of the company. Bob describes one of the measures they were forced to take: "We actually sent a telegram to the landlords saying we're not paying full rent; if we were paying one thousand dollars a month, we were only going to pay six hundred dollars. We said we need to lower the rent, and then we'll pay you back over the balance of the lease. And they all said, 'What if we don't do it?' My answer was, 'Well, then we go broke.' They didn't have much in the way of an alternative. At least if they complied with our proposal, they had a chance of getting their money back eventually. So it was better for them to take the chance and do it." All of them agreed to go along with the company's offer because 50 percent of something was better than 100 percent of nothing.

While the company was renegotiating leases, John steeled himself to renegotiate the terms of the loan with John Hancock. He assured them that he had every intention of paying off all he owed; he just needed time. They did renegotiate, with very stringent restrictions on how Der Wienerschnitzel was to conduct business. Among the restrictions were limits on purchasing or opening new stands and a requirement that the company maintain a certain net worth for a period of two years. Hancock knew it was better to receive their money over time than take a loss by pushing Der Wienerschnitzel into bankruptcy. John agreed to the terms, which gave the company a little breathing room. There was still the problem of those stores that were losing money on a daily basis. The slow climb out of debt would take months, if not years, and John knew that many stores would be forced to close as a result of the imminent belt-tightening.

Through it all, John worked hard to keep his cool, shelter his home life from the stress he was under, and provide a positive, upbeat attitude for his staff and associates. Unavoidably, there were people who got hurt, and that resulted in one particularly frightening episode when a disgruntled owner of a failed store walked into John's office brandishing a gun. John, who had proven his ability to remain calm in the face of disaster, said very little. Instead, he listened intently and let the man talk until he had his say. Who could have anticipated that John's ability to listen could save his life? But this time it did. The owner put away his gun and left satisfied that he had been able to talk to the head of the company, which was really all he came for. John was aware of how differently it all might have turned out, not only for himself, but for others in the office, if he had countered the intruder with aggression. Instead, John used his calm demeanor to literally dodge a bullet.

Calmness was a trait Dick Hodge first noticed in John when they were on a trip together. "We were in Boston for the financing deal with John Hancock, and we were at a bar one night after the meeting, and I got into an argument with some guy standing at the bar next to me. I was getting really excited about it, and John was like, 'No, no, Dick. No, no, let's just forget about it.' He grabs me and walks me out of the bar. That's how he was in any situation; he never became too excited. And he was a great reader of people. He could understand people and figure out what they needed. He had a great gift for getting along with lots of different people."

Thanks to John's tenacity and the hard work of everyone involved, the company started moving away from the financial precipice, but so slowly that there was still no end to their losses in sight. They did everything in their power to promote the image of Der Wienerschnitzel as a viable and growing enterprise. They launched an aggressive public relations campaign and participated in conventions and regional trade events that recognized successful franchisees.

National conventions became key to bringing the Der Wienerschnitzel family together and keeping morale high. And any bit of good news was embraced to the maximum.

Even in the midst of all the doom and gloom, there was occasionally a ray of hope. Certain stores continued to show profits, and the owners had confidence in John as a trusted leader. One night, while John was checking the monthly income from all the stores, he noticed that one store in particular, in Fresno, California, was having an unusual spike in sales. The following day, he met with Bob Trujillo to show him the figures. Both men decided it was something they needed to check out. Maybe this owner was doing something they should know about. John dispatched his trusted associate Kirk Robison to take a look at the Fresno store to see what the owner was up to. Two days later, the word came back. The Fresno store was offering a special giveaway: "Buy a Coke. Keep the glass."

The store owner had purchased a large number of classic Coke glasses and was giving them away with the purchase of a Coca-Cola. It was the first time a giveaway of that kind had been introduced in the fast-food industry. It was proving to be an extremely popular promotion, and the return traffic was enormous, because customers weren't satisfied with just one glass—they wanted a whole set. That was exactly the kind of return business Der Wienerschnitzel needed in order to establish a loyal customer base. This was John's kind of franchisee—a man who had found a way to stay within the boundaries of the company guidelines and add a clever idea that accomplished the most important objective in business: dramatically increasing sales and profits. The idea was a cheap investment that resulted in big returns!

John quickly allotted $6,000 for marketing and advertising and launched the "Buy a Coke. Keep the glass." promotion throughout the entire Der Wienerschnitzel chain. This was the turning point. It was so successful that in 1973, the company sold 15 million Cokes as part of the giveaway marketing strategy, which jump-started the entire company and finally turned things around for the better. The dark clouds of the past few years had started to recede, and up ahead, the sun was shining.

If John hadn't paid special attention to the numbers at one of the two hundred stores, the situation could have turned out very differently. John had dug himself out of a deep hole through perseverance, optimism, a bit of good luck, and a heck of a lot of Coca-Cola glasses. It had been a roller coaster, but the company was now back on track, and things were gathering speed. As for the John Hancock debt, John paid it off in full. And as a result, his stellar credit standing with John Hancock remained intact his entire life.

Coke adds life and profit to Der Wienerschnitzel with promo.

The Times featuring Wienerschnitzel

Project 80

6

By the early 1970s, John Galardi could breathe a deep sigh of relief. The decade had been a proving ground for Der Wienerschnitzel, and John had made it through with flying colors. The worst of times seemed to be behind him, even though there were still seismic changes on the political, economic, and cultural landscape.

Worldwide inflation raised the price of gasoline, food, and manufacturing. In the United States, the rate of inflation topped 11 percent.

While he wasn't on the run, John was reinventing himself and taking advantage of his hard-earned recovery. His success had lit a flame that went far and above pure business interests. You could say he started to live a little. He discovered in himself a bit of the showman, and a desire to own "big-boy toys"—

which he carried over into flamboyant marketing strategies for Der Wienerschnitzel and his personal life.

Speed and fun were all part of John's orientation toward life and business. He decided that a great publicity venture for Der Wienerschnitzel would be to sponsor race cars. He loved to go to the track and watch the sleek machines zipping by so fast he could hardly read the words "Der Wienerschnitzel" painted on the side.

John's lifestyle was that of someone young and successful, but it took a toll on his family life. He reveled in going out to clubs to drink with buddies and, of course, business associates. Even though his family had always been his top priority, he didn't always turn up for dinner. And he wasn't great at attending PTA meetings, school-related activities, or even important family celebrations.

By the end of 1974, Der Wienerschnitzel's revenues and expenses were under control, and the company generated a net income of over $1 million. Now the company had 57 leased or company-owned restaurants and 134 franchised restaurants after jettisoning the losing stores from their inventory.

That same year, John directed his architects to come up with a new design for the Der Wienerschnitzel stores. The project was dubbed "The Concept 80," signifying that the stores would have a fresh, new look for the next decade, and a design that responded to changing consumer tastes. The Concept 80 offered inside seating at certain sites rather than just drive-thru service. It also boasted better kitchen facilities and a higher-quality drive-thru arrangement. The new design was in response to market research, which showed that many customers wanted a place to sit and eat at the store rather than just pick up a meal at the drive-thru and leave. The other noticeable change was the replacement of the runner-chargers with speaker boxes that greeted you and took your order.

Although the old A-frame remained a sentimental favorite with many customers, The Concept 80 went into production as sales figures continued to climb. John expressed his gratitude to all the people who had stuck with him and helped him turn the company around by instituting a profit-sharing plan for his permanent corporate employees. In the first year of the program, $111,217 were distributed.

The money was finally rolling in, but unlike the freewheeling sixties, John insisted on strict financial controls to make sure that growth would be carefully managed by a team that reported directly to him.

By 1976, any pending litigation from the public offering debacle had been resolved, and the company assets increased by $1 million. Working capital exceeded $3 million. The company's balance sheet was healthy, and the *Mustard Sheet*—the in-house newsletter—was printing all good news. John felt it was time to make another big move.

Bob Trujillo recalls a company meeting where John discussed the idea of moving the entire company from its offices in Torrance to a bigger office in Newport Beach, forty miles away. No one was in favor of it. The entire corporate staff was settled in Torrance, with the exception of John. They owned homes in Torrance; their children were in school there; and the idea of an eighty-mile round-trip commute sounded dismal. John listened attentively to everyone's objections.

Two weeks later, he announced that they were moving the corporate offices to Newport Beach.

As difficult as it was for many, eventually everyone made the transition. This was a testament to their trust in John and their willingness to follow him to the ends of the earth. Some complained, but when the move was completed, everyone admitted it'd been the right thing to do. The new surroundings were beautiful, and the change boosted company morale. Sales kept climbing, heading to nearly $5 million annually.

The demands of Der Wienerschnitzel continued to take a toll on the Galardis' family life. In order to maintain control over company operations in the field, John was constantly traveling.

Balancing home life with his desire for success was becoming even more difficult for John. His personal life was imploding. However, Der Wienerschnitzel continued to grow and now boasted 265 stores in twenty-two states. It was projected to reach a total of 365 stores by 1979. In the spirit of continued innovation, John considered changing the standard Der Wienerschnitzel menu by adding hamburgers. The idea might have seemed sacrilege to some, but John was well aware that in the fast-food world, hamburgers were the number-one-selling item. He didn't want to compete head-to-head with any of the fast-food hamburger chains; he just wanted to broaden Der Wienerschnitzel's appeal. If a family of four came in and one of them didn't want hot dogs, they were liable to lose all four customers. So "mouth-watering hamburgers" were added to the menu in 1977.

Unfortunately, hamburgers didn't take off in a big way and accounted for only 6 percent of sales. But they did have the desired effect of appealing to a wider customer base. Whether they would succeed in the long run remained unknown, but the company committed itself wholeheartedly to the concept. It was certainly a departure from the company's core menu—everything hot dogs—but it was, to John, a gamble worth taking.

A national television ad campaign was launched with this catchy jingle:

You're looking for a place to eat with friends and family,
Some say burgers, some say hot dogs, no one can agree.
Head to Wienerschnitzel, we're all together now,
With hamburgers and hot dogs, no more need to look around.
With hamburgers and hot dogs, it's all together now.
At Der Wienerschnitzel, it's all together now.
At Der Wienerschnitzel!

During these years, John tried to throw himself into work, but he realized he needed more help when that work caused

the dissolution of his marriage to Myrna. He made a decision he thought would be best for the company—he stepped down from his role as president on October 28, 1977, and became the CEO of Der Wienerschnitzel, appointing Bob Trujillo as president in his place to take over the day-to-day operations. He was confident the company would be in safe hands with Bob while he was far away trying to regain some balance in his life—on a boat in the Bahamas.

John Galardi needed a complete change of scenery.

Illustration of the new Concept 80 design.

Renaissance Man

7

John decided the Bahamas was a prime place to reset. The beach and open air would allow him the much-needed breather he wanted in order to come to terms with his divorce. He also thought it was time to assess what the future of the business might look like. He was never more than a phone call away from Bob, now president of Der Wienerschnitzel, and stayed involved remotely with everything that was happening at corporate. Along with the revamping of his personal life, he had the feeling his company could use one as well. He set his sights on a new look for the logo.

John had met the famous graphic designer Saul Bass, who was responsible for some of Hollywood's best-known movie posters: *West Side Story*, *Spartacus*, *It's a Mad, Mad, Mad, Mad World*, and *Exodus*. He also created some of the most recognizable corporate logos for Quaker, AT&T, and United Airlines. When John asked Bass to design a logo for Der Wienerschnitzel, he said, "It's going to cost you one hundred thousand dollars." John replied, "I only have ten thousand dollars." Apparently, Bass must have liked John, because he agreed to the much lower price. He did say, however, that he would accept it on the condition that there would be no change to his design. He also wanted to drop the *Der*. Bass told John the company needed a strong, recognizable logo, and the *Der* diluted the impact of what he intended to design. Just like that, Wienerschnitzel (without the *Der*) was reborn.

Some say Saul Bass's inspiration for the logo came from a hot dog and a squiggle of mustard. Clearly, the whole was greater than the sum of its parts, because the Saul Bass-designed logo is still used by the company to this day. Hot off the drawing board and with John's strong endorsement, the clean, hip, and easily recognizable design replaced the old Der Wienerschnitzel lettering with its Tyrolean vibe. The fresh logo would eventually even find its way onto drinking cups, baseball caps, French fry holders, and napkins. It became the catchy trademark the brand needed and that John had always wanted.

In 1979, John finally returned from his stay in the Bahamas, ready to dive back into work. Wienerschnitzel was a well-oiled machine and thriving, so he found himself searching for something else to jump into. He looked at new and diversified business interests. According to his friends and business associates, John wanted to recapture the excitement and adrenaline rush of another start-up venture, so he tried his hand at a number of different businesses. He invested in several nightclubs and discos, including the Jockey Club and Tiffany's in Newport Beach. While in this scene, he met a new group of guys to hang out with who were unlike his business associates at Wienerschnitzel. These men, whether single or married, were into heavy partying, which John had never been part of before.

Richard Hodge describes John's state of mind at that time: "He surrounded himself with people he thought were entertaining. He liked their sense of humor or their taste in women or whatever it may be. He was a Renaissance man in the sense that he was interested in everything. The emphasis became different depending on where he was in his personal journey through life, but he had broad interests other than his business. He was interested in all kinds of things. He had great strengths, tenderness, generosity, love, and kindness, but what drove him was this incredible curiosity about the world. He was from a small town in Missouri, and by this time, he was aware of the great big world, and he wanted to throw his arms around it."

***

In the world of business, the worst financial recession since the 1930s hit the United States and spread worldwide in the early '80s. It was prompted by rapid price fluctuations in the oil market, which was followed by a hike in interest rates from 11 to 20 percent. The unemployment rate rose from 5.6 to 7.5 percent. The deregulation of banking brought about an initial surge in real estate, which ended up collapsing under the weight of bad loans. Banks started closing, and with their financial futures uncertain, Americans started tightening their belts.

Eating out was considered a luxury for many, and even though fast-food restaurants were inexpensive, they, too, felt the pinch of the recession. At the same time, Wienerschnitzel was on a building spree with many new stores set to open. John had to step back in to take charge because of the sociological and financial issues facing America. His focus was on restoring the company to a solid footing. Karen remembers, "It wasn't as if any of us had to move into a cheaper house, or we had to get rid of the cars, nothing like that. Dad always made sure that our lives totally stayed the same, but I'm sure he went through some very stressful times."

What the economic downturn did trigger, though, were some major personnel changes at Wienerschnitzel. For the good of the company, John had to let go of a number of longtime friends who had worked for him for many years.

It was a difficult and painful time of transition, but John found a way to make it a tad less painful. All the original Wienerschnitzel team, including Ron Bryant, Kirk Robison, Paul Hironimus, Carl Evans, and Bill Linder, were given multiple stores that would guarantee them financial security for the rest of their lives. In addition, many of their children, who had worked in the stands since their teenage years, would become second-generation franchisees. It was John's way of taking care of the whole family, something he had done from the very beginning.

By 1981, all the trimming had put the company in better shape financially, so Bob Trujillo decided it was the right time for him to leave and focus on developing his real estate business with Bill Linder. In Bob's words: "When I said 'John, I'm going to leave,' he asked, 'Well, what do you want?' I replied, 'I don't know.' John thought for a moment and said, 'Take anything you want.' So he gave me a year's salary, a pension, a car, and five franchises. That guy would do anything for me. When I left, he sent me and my whole family to Hawaii because of what I had done for him." That's John for you.

When Bob stepped down, John moved back into the role of president, but he didn't go to headquarters on a daily basis since he could work remotely. He could review the company's financials from anywhere, since he had the ability to analyze performance reports and consolidated statements quickly and directly after so many years of practice.

John's management team included Chief Financial Officer Alan Fuller, whom John had worked with since the late 1970s; Vice President of Operations Gene Howell, who had come to Wienerschnitzel from Wendy's; and Marketing Director Dennis Tase, the latest addition, who had been hired from PepsiCo, where he'd worked in marketing and operations. John hit it off well with Dennis. Dennis recalls, "John was a closet marketing guy; a very good marketing guy, actually. He wasn't well educated in it. He just had the right instincts for what should be done from a marketing perspective. When I accepted the job, I told my wife 'I'm not going to be here very long,' but then John and I got along great, and I realized I really enjoyed working for this guy. I had a couple of opportunities to go some other places, and I thought maybe I would move on, but I never did."

***

John's life was about to undergo some major changes, including a vacation to Hawaii where he met his new love interest, the radiant Cindy Palmer. Their connection was immediate. Back home from vacation, John and Cindy discovered they both lived in Newport Beach, so they started dating regularly. Their relationship flourished as they drew closer, and Cindy told John she wanted to have children. John already had two daughters and considered that part of his life closed, so he told her no. Cindy responded by telling him goodbye and walking out the door.

This transition was hard for John. Because he and Cindy lived in the same city, he saw her out on dates with other men from time to time, and quickly decided he couldn't be without her. John reached out to Cindy and conceded to having children if it meant he could be with her. She accepted and they resumed dating for two years before getting married at Laguna Beach.

Other adventures naturally revolved around business, and so once again, John dove into forming a game plan for the future. He called upon his vice president of marketing, John Douglas, to come up with ideas. Douglas proposed a number of options, but none of them were the right fit. Finally, after many of them were left on the cutting-room floor, they hit upon Photo Works, a new concept for developing and delivering photos in a one-hour turnaround.

John hired Bob Trujillo's son, Tom, to launch Photo Works and oversee the whole project from start to finish. Tom recalls, "John was looking for a way to upgrade the newer Wienerschnitzel stores that were nonperforming and close some of the older A-frames. And now John could approach certain franchisees and tell them, 'Listen, we're not going to keep you on as a Wienerschnitzel franchisee; we're going to ask you to consider running another business, Photo Works.' He was optimistic that everything would work out."

Tom continues, "We thought we could take our multiunit expertise and just transfer it into the photo business. But the one-hour photo business had a very different customer base from the Wienerschnitzel customer base. John projected opening ten Photo Works. We only managed to open three, and the entire operation folded in just over a year. Adding up the expenses for reconfiguring store interiors, new equipment, marketing, and advertising, John lost about a million dollars on this venture. But he was fine with it. John was a black-and-white kind of guy. I remember John telling me, 'Tommy, shut them down and get out! Let me know what you're going to do next.' John was already on to another franchise possibility, The Original Hamburger Stand."

The Original Hamburger Stand was going to be unlike the previous low-key addition of hamburgers to the Wienerschnitzel menu back in the late 1970s.

Starting Hamburger Stand was a direct assault on the established fast-food hamburger chains such as In-N-Out Burger, McDonald's, Jack in the Box, and Burger King. The Hamburger Stand offered low-priced, no-frills hamburgers at twenty-nine cents, and its locations were often set up in poorly performing Wienerschnitzel A-frame stores. The packaging for the food was generic, with plainly labeled items like "Bag," "Cup," and "Burger" rather than expensive brand labels and colorful wrappers. Their competitors had to drastically drop their prices to keep up, and that's what started the Burger Wars so long ago.

John's idea had worked, and suddenly he had a moderately successful alternative venture on his hands. Once a number of stores were up and running, he decided to open another small chain, Weldon's Gourmet Hamburgers, which offered a more upscale menu of gourmet hamburgers.

Wienerschnitzel was once again thriving and didn't require John's constant attention, so in 1984, he decided to step away from the daily governing of the company. Dennis Tase, who had been running the marketing department with such a steady hand, was appointed vice president and general manager of the Wienerschnitzel division as well as the Hamburger Stand. However, John remained president and CEO of the parent company and its highly diversified operations. John described this transition in a press interview: "I'll be the coach, and Dennis will be my quarterback." Dennis seconds that statement: "He truly was a coach. There was no question about it. I used to tell him that when I was at Pepsi, I thought the CEO, John Sculley, was one of the best I've ever seen at presenting ideas to people. John Galardi could have made Sculley look like a novice. I mean, the man was brilliant when it came to getting people to do the things he wanted them to do. The other great thing about John was that he believed in family. It was one of the reasons that I stayed. When I worked for Pepsi, I didn't have any time for my family. When I came to work with Wienerschnitzel, if I wanted to go coach my kid for baseball, John didn't have any problem with that, and the next day he'd ask, 'How was the game? How did your kid do?'"

By 1984, there were 322 stores in a dozen states nationwide that generated a steady stream of income. By 1986, the coach and quarterback were on a winning streak. Dennis always praised John's management style: "He believed in a fundamental of our industry: the business starts at the store level, and if it works at one store, it will work at other stores. So we tested things, and we stayed focused. Even when I first started, I realized that if our franchisees are not profitable, then we can't do anything. We can't go anywhere. So closing stores and opening other stores wasn't the overall goal, it was to maintain profitability throughout the entire universe of Wienerschnitzel."

In 1986, with three separate franchise ventures up and running (Wienerschnitzel, The Original Hamburger Stand, and Weldon's Gourmet Hamburgers) and further diversification on the drawing board, John changed the name of the parent company from Wienerschnitzel to the Galardi Group and named Dennis Tase president.

In the background of all these developing restaurants, John and Cindy had tried and failed to have children of their own. They turned to adoption and brought their daughter, Skylar, home to stay. One year later, a miracle happened when Cindy became pregnant. On January 18, 1989, she and John welcomed their son, John Ross "JR" Galardi into their lives.

In that same year, there was also rapid growth in the Galardi Group. In order for John to maintain the semiretired status he was enjoying, he needed to reorganize his upper-management staff. He changed his own title to chairman and CEO, and promoted Dennis Tase to president and chief operating officer.

Dennis handled the day-to-day operations, but the critical big-picture decisions were John's and always would be. He could never fully take his hands off the wheel of the business, but promoting Dennis did give him a chance to spend more time with Cindy and the kids. It gave him the license to enjoy his family more and to participate in celebrations that he had missed in the past.

Neither John nor Cindy believed in spoiling the children. They wanted them to work for what they had and be grounded, but those were difficult lessons to teach after moving to Aspen, Colorado, a permanent resort town. The children always had chores and received allowance money, which they could spend on personal items. When JR was six years old, he desperately wanted a snowboard, but he didn't have enough saved to buy it. So he devised a clever plan. He bought newspapers at a quarter apiece and sold them around town. Because he was just six, most people gave him at least a dollar. JR was obviously already showing signs of his father's entrepreneurial spirit.

Cindy remembers, "We had log fencing around our property that had to be oiled. It was really toxic. You couldn't get it on your hands or arms, and you had to wear a mask over your face. So there was JR at ten or eleven years old, in the heat of summer, hard at work on the fence. All our friends would be driving back and forth from town past our property, and they saw this little kid working away on the fence. They couldn't tell it was JR, because he was totally covered up.

"They asked, 'Who's that oiling your fence?' And of course I said, 'That's JR.' It was miserable work, but he wanted to make money, so he did it. He was very determined to get what he wanted, and neither John nor I were just going to give him a handout. We told all the kids that when they turned sixteen, we would match whatever money they had saved for a car. To our surprise, JR had saved eight thousand dollars. We matched it, and JR bought an Audi!"

It wasn't all work and no play, though. Skylar followed in the footsteps of her half-sisters, Teresa and Karen, and had her own horse, which she rode in competitions. JR joined the school hockey team and made his dad proud by winning many medals. During the winter, Skylar and JR went skiing or snowboarding every day. They were active and determined children. Despite what may have seemed like a privileged life, JR recalls, "Most of my classmates at school in Aspen were the children of the 'regular' townspeople. Their parents ran the local stores, worked in construction, staffed the hotels, and so forth. They weren't the children of the 'fancy' vacationers who flew in on their private jets for two weeks in the winter and summer. It was really a very normal environment without a lot of pretense."

As the children flourished, John continued dividing his time between Aspen and Newport. Cindy focused her energy on volunteer work in the Aspen community, where her business and organizational skills were greatly appreciated, and she was tapped to be on the board of several charitable organizations. It is often said, though, that if you achieve your goals, you haven't set them high enough. Despite everything the Galardis had already accomplished, after seventeen years of marriage, they decided that it was time to travel the world in order to give Skylar and JR the cultural enrichment that visiting foreign countries provided. Other family members, including Cindy's mother, Lillian, and John's mother, Virginia, also often participated in these trips. John was the patriarch of a large family that loved and honored him. His family shared his values, respected his accomplishments, and appreciated his generosity. It didn't get much better than that for him.

In 1998, when Skylar was eleven and JR nine, Karen gave birth to a son, Liam Winston. Now John was blessed with the joy of seeing the Galardi family expand into the next generation, and experienced the special love that only a grandchild can bring. The 1990s were wonderful years for the Galardis. John was grateful for all that he had accomplished, and it gave him great pleasure to share the rewards of success with the people he loved.

As the twentieth century drew to a close, America was in a time of social and political unrest. The second term of the extremely popular president Bill Clinton was riddled by personal scandal, and the North American Free Trade Agreement, which had been enacted by Congress in 1994, was now being viewed as a decimator of American jobs. Nevertheless, the stock market crossed the ten thousand mark for the first time in US economic history, despite all the political and economic turmoil. With that historic milestone, the Wienerschnitzel franchise continued to grow, and so did the Galardi clan. Cindy's nephews, Robert and Eric, needed a place to live, and John welcomed them in with open arms. They, too, were family.

Fortunately, the international school that JR and Skylar were attending also believed that travel was just as important as classroom education. Their homework consisted of making a photographic journal of their travels to Egypt, Morocco, Spain, Italy, India, England, and all over France. Now the world was truly John's oyster, and he was sharing the pearls with his wife and children. Cindy reminisced:

"In an Indian village, the residents celebrated the first day of spring by spraying each other with water-based paint. People could be in suits or saris—it didn't matter. Everyone was fair game. It was all in good fun. Some kids invited JR to come out with them, and he hopped on the back of a bike with a young boy who gave him his water gun. JR went through town spraying everyone with paint. Then he got sprayed and came back completely drenched with paint. A band marched through the street, and everyone started dancing. Naturally, we all joined in. On every trip we took, we went off the beaten path and saw and did things that were not available to tourists who were on standard organized tours. We always had a great time, and it was certainly educational for Skylar and JR—and for John and me as well."

Later, in 1999, after ten adventurous months in Europe, the Galardis finally returned to Aspen. During his time abroad, John was able to stay in close touch by phone or telex with

Dennis Tase and was kept in the loop with company issues. Fortunately, it was a seamlessly smooth working relationship. As Dennis explains, "I always bounced stuff off of John. It's not like there was an edict that said he had to approve of everything. I just felt that we were a team, and we worked well together. I knew what he liked, and I wasn't going to create something knowing in advance that he wouldn't like it, which is why he never said no. We were a great team."

As a result of their staying in contact and their great relationship, there were no surprises awaiting John when he returned. The company remained on a steady upward climb, spurred by the introduction of a popular new menu item: soft-serve treats. That year, the company also entered into a licensing agreement with Tastee-Freez International to sell soft-serve ice cream in Wienerschnitzel and Hamburger Stand restaurants. It was the most successful dessert item the company had ever introduced, and within three years, it would add $2 million per year to the chain-wide sales.

It was another huge—and unexpected—win for all.

John Galardi and his new wife, Cindy, with their children, Skylar and JR.

True Commitment

8

As the ball dropped in Times Square, heralding the start of a new millennium, the global fears of a Y2K meltdown never materialized. In fact, the American economy was on a roll at the start of 2000, and Wienerschnitzel and Hamburger Stand were along for the ride. Weldon's hadn't proven as profitable, so John wisely dropped it after a few years. The Galardi Group now boasted 334 stores with many more in the planning stages.

An interesting and positive change in the company over the years was the profile of franchisees. It had changed dramatically, from predominantly US-born owners to recent immigrants from China, Korea, India, Cuba, and the Middle East. These franchisees had come to America with a good education, dreams of a better life, and a real commitment to hard work.

John embraced the change. His pride in these members of the Wienerschnitzel family reflected his own family's dreams and ambitions not many years prior. These were good people— people like Farouk Diab.

An Israeli-born Palestinian, Farouk came to America in 1975. Farouk had grown up with the kind of discipline that came from working long hours on his father's farm in Israel. A cousin who had moved to the States painted such a glowing picture of life in America that in August 1975, Farouk took a leap of faith and left behind his family and Sahira, the girl he hoped to marry, to come to San Jose, California, with barely enough money to last three months. Farouk was nineteen years old and, just as John Galardi had done in 1958, he went knocking door to door looking for any kind of work. All he needed was the opportunity and a little bit of luck. And that's just what Farouk found when he walked into Der Wienerschnitzel in San Jose. The owner, George Kreiten, recognized Farouk's accent, because George was also from Israel. That lucky coincidence created an instant bond between the two men. Kreiten hired Farouk on the spot, with apologies that, right now, all he could offer was janitorial work at the minimum wage, $1.60 an hour. Farouk jumped at the chance.

Farouk showed such dedication that, after eight months, George took him off janitorial duties and installed him full-time in the kitchen where, according to Farouk, he "worked his tail off every single day." Within a year, Farouk was promoted to night manager and then to day manager. After two years, Farouk was generating the highest sales the store had ever earned. George Kreiten recommended to the home office that Farouk become an owner of a franchise: the beginning of an amazing career that saw Farouk Diab rise from a job as a janitor to one of the most successful franchisees in Wienerschnitzel history. In 1980, five years after he arrived in the US, Farouk went back to Israel and brought his bride, Sahira, back to San Jose, where they would build a life together on a solid financial footing.

Over the next forty years, Farouk acquired over twenty-two stores. He and Sahira raised six children, and two of them are now company district managers. Farouk was one of many people who, through Wienerschnitzel, achieved not only the American Dream, but also John Galardi's dream—that Wienerschnitzel would remain a family-oriented company and that others would follow in his footsteps to make a better life for themselves and their families. In 2015, the magazine *Multi-Unit Franchisee* gave Farouk Diab its Most Valuable Performer Award.

Equally inspiring is the story of Steve Ham, who in 1976, arrived in America with his parents from Seoul, South Korea. Steve was twenty-three years old and enlisted in the US Army to serve his new country as an infantryman. He worked his way up to a desk job in the supplies division. After serving six years, Steve began looking for some kind of business that could support him, his wife Teresa, and their two young daughters. While reading a Korean-American newspaper, he found an offer that looked interesting. It was for the sale of a Wienerschnitzel franchise in Santa Ana, California. With the wind in his sails, Steve made the forty-mile trip from Los Angeles to see the store. He liked what he saw and made an offer, which was accepted. Steve had never worked in the restaurant business, but his army training had taught him discipline and a willingness to work hard, the two most important ingredients for success.

On September 21, 1982, Steve Ham opened his first store in Santa Ana and quickly became an award-winning franchisee. Wienerschnitzel provided Steve with such a successful business opportunity that he was able to expand his franchise and open three other stores, which are still doing great business today. He enlisted other family members as franchisees, and the Ham family currently owns seven stores operated by Steve, his brother, his sister, and his sister-in-law. It is a real family affair.

***

John's vision of passing the torch from one generation to the next is exemplified in the story of Esther Beard and her daughters. Esther—Bob Trujillo's sister—and her husband were among the earliest franchisees. After her husband passed away at the age of fifty-nine, Esther continued operating their stores on a daily basis until she was in her eighties.

Two of her four daughters also became franchisees. Her daughter Carol Ecker tells this story: "My twin sister Cheryl and I started working at Der Wienerschnitzel when we were eleven years old. We were not even able to reach the drink station and had to stand on ice buckets to make the fountain drinks. Our parents taught us that we would have to help pay for our college educations, so by the time we were teenagers, we were working the drive-thru and the front registers. We were required to go out to the car in the drive-thru, completely memorize their order, and add up the sum in our heads. It was hard, but we got really good at it. My sister and I went off to college swearing that we would never get into the family business. Well, that didn't last long. My sister and I became the youngest franchisees in the company's history. I purchased my first Wienerschnitzel at the age of twenty-one. Today, we've both been in the Wienerschnitzel franchise for thirty-seven years."

To John Galardi, the franchisees are the heart of the Wienerschnitzel family.

They invest their hopes, their dreams, their finances, and their lives to help make the company successful. It is a true commitment of faith, trust, and, yes, love.

What John gave them in return is the chance to have a thriving business as true entrepreneurs and pass something valuable along to their children, even their grandchildren.

Former COO and President Dennis Tase agrees: "The future of the company is the franchisees. If everyone in corporate left, the franchisees would continue. Their strength and dedication are the backbone of Wienerschnitzel."

Farouk Diab on the cover of the September 2015 issue of Multi-Unit Franchisee magazine for Wienerschnitzel.

A franchisee's eternal love for Wienerschnitzel—no further caption needed!

American Dreamer

9

September 11, 2001, was a dark day for all Americans. John was in New York City with Cindy and Karen. John and Cindy had just settled Skylar into a boarding school in upstate New York and were in their hotel room packing to return to Aspen. At 8:46 a.m., the world changed forever. The first of two jetliners struck the Twin Towers at the World Trade Center on Manhattan's Lower East Side, shattering any illusion that the United States was immune to a terrorist attack.

The news of the day kept getting worse as an attack on the Pentagon was reported, then another jetliner went down over Pennsylvania, reportedly headed for the nation's capital. Cindy recalls, "There was no leaving New York, and the only way we could think to help was to donate blood. We went out hoping to find a cab to take us to a hospital, but the streets were completely empty, not a single car. The smell of burning debris was still in the air, and fighter jets were flying overhead. It was like being in a war zone. The city was completely immobilized. We finally made our way to a hospital but were turned away. There was nothing we could do. We had to go back to the hotel and wait three days before we were finally able to charter a private plane to get out."

Like millions of other Americans, John was stunned by this unspeakable tragedy that claimed more than 3,500 lives and injured many more. The financial markets, which had dropped two thousand points on that fateful day, went into a further tailspin in November when a US energy group, Enron Corporation, collapsed, filing for the biggest bankruptcy reorganization in corporate history.

This was a tough time to carry on. But John knew he had responsibilities to his family and to the wider Wienerschnitzel family. The Galardi Group experienced internal shifts when longtime Chief Financial Officer, Alan Fuller, retired. Fortunately, waiting in the wings to assume the title was Controller Ken Wagstaff, who'd been with the company since 1987. It was a smooth transition.

Wienerschnitzel experienced a burst of good fortune as sales of Tastee-Freez soared. Rather than continuing license-fee payments to the company, COO Dennis Tase made a decision to acquire Tastee-Freez outright. He negotiated a fair price and brought the offer to John. The two men took a trip to Michigan to meet with the Tastee-Freez owner to finalize the deal. Dennis's recollection of that meeting is priceless: "I was sitting in the room, and John said to this guy, 'Have you ever sold any companies before?' The guy says, 'No,' and John says, 'Well, I have, and you're not taking this into consideration, you're not taking that into consideration, and so this is what we're going to do with the price.' And we ended up paying more than the price I had negotiated. That shows you the passion that John Galardi had. He wanted to make a good deal, but at the same time, he wanted to make sure that you understood what you were doing."

The new CFO, Ken Wagstaff, greatly admired John's negotiation process. "He was an old throwback guy, a handshake guy. When John shook your hand, that's all you needed; you didn't need to make sure you had it in writing or needed him to sign off. He was a very straightforward, plainspoken guy. A very bright guy, obviously. He had a great knack for seeing a complex situation and boiling it down to the simple issues that needed to be resolved. I'm a very detail-oriented person, so I'm constantly looking at this giant spreadsheet and trying to put all the facts together, and John could just say, 'Well, these are the three things that we need to worry about.' When adversity struck, that's when he got down to working. I think he liked a challenge, he liked to solve problems. He used to say, 'Solving problems is the fuel of life.'"

Over the next ten years, Tastee-Freez became a real favorite with customers.

Annual soft-serve dessert sales climbed to almost $19 million by the end of 2016.

Dennis Tase credits much of the company's success to an innovative marketing strategy and advertising campaign. "One of the best things we ever did was, we went to a small agency called DGWB. They were four full partners, and they were a hungry agency and very creative. Truly, they put us on the map. In fact, Doug Koegeboehn, the guy who was instrumental in helping us at DGWB, is now in charge of marketing at the Galardi Group."

DGWB created new and innovative campaigns for television and radio, including a memorable ad campaign featuring the well-known Delicious One, the anthropomorphic chili-dog character who became known as "The World's Most Wanted Wiener." That slogan inspired television ads in which the Delicious One was always being chased by adoring fans as he ran from them screaming, with the tagline, "They'll do almost anything to get their hands on him." Dennis Tase rolled out the new ad campaign at an annual convention, which he'd learned was a way to spark enthusiasm with the franchisees. Everyone loved it. The campaign was a big success, and the character became a pop icon with fans and collectors of memorabilia depicting the Delicious One's frantic efforts to escape from being eaten by hungry customers. Wienerschnitzel adopted the Delicious One as the company's official mascot, so he was seen not only in TV commercials, but also at thousands of events promoting the brand over the years.

In 2011, Wienerschnitzel celebrated its fiftieth anniversary, touting it in print and other media. It was certainly something to be proud of. John had proven he was great at pulling the strings behind a successful company. For many years, he'd resisted the idea of appearing in a television commercial, but that year he finally relented. For the first time, the public got to see the top dog behind the magic of Wienerschnitzel. Performing wasn't really such a big stretch for John, who had always exhibited a fun-loving side by dressing up for costume parties. And, as everyone already knew, he was always eager to try something new.

There were a few dark clouds during this time too, and overwhelming success again kept John away from those closest to him: his immediate family. It put a lot of pressure on his marriage to Cindy. They tried to work things out, but life had taken them in different directions. Cindy recalls fondly, "We had many wonderful years . . . At some point, as the children grew older, our lives started going different directions. We grew apart. When JR, our youngest, was leaving for college, we decided we had little in common, and our marriage ended . . . My heart hurts every day for our children." Despite the divorce in 2009, both Cindy and John remained devoted parents to Skylar, JR, Robert, and Eric.

***

For several years, John's health had been on the decline. In 2011, at age seventy-two, he examined his life and came to the realization that the demon he had been running from all these years was not poverty or abandonment, it was the certainty that life must end; in the words of the English poet W. H. Auden, "Death is the sound of distant thunder at a picnic." John recognized his days were coming to an end. He was keenly aware that he needed to create a succession plan and leave the reins of Wienerschnitzel in capable hands. He never demanded his children follow in his footsteps, but he had always hoped that one day, JR would become part of Wienerschnitzel.

After graduating from the University of Colorado Denver with a degree in music business, JR had successfully launched his own concert promotion business in Colorado with a partner. He credits his work ethic to his upbringing. "I always wanted to work. I like the feeling of achieving something. I got that from my parents. I tell people I won the genetic lottery; I was blessed in everything I got. I'm just trying to do my best with it."

John always loved talking business with his son. JR recalls riding in the car as a child, listening to his father share whatever business issues were on his mind, as if JR were an adult. When John and Cindy separated, JR would go to Newport to spend time with his father and work as an intern in various divisions of the company. "I started as a janitor in one of the restaurants. Years later, I moved to a low-level marketing position, and I would go to every regional market, do all the presentations, and report back to my dad how everything went. From there, I became an operator and went through thirteen weeks of training. I ran the store in Newport, where I had worked as a janitor at thirteen years old."

In 2011, John encouraged JR to stay in Southern California on a more permanent basis so the two could spend time together. JR recalls, "I spent two days a week with my dad around the clock, going to meetings, listening to how he would analyze a situation and how he would deal with problems. Then Dad would ask me if I agreed with what he'd done or if I had any ideas to improve upon it." In a subtle but deliberate way, John was testing the waters to see if JR was ready to take on more responsibility.

Cindy was aware of John's master plan to eventually hand the baton off to JR. "Even though in the last four years of John's life I didn't live with him, he was still a huge presence in my life, in everyone's life. You could always rely on John. Of course, we had our disagreements when we were getting divorced, but you never stop loving somebody, no matter what the situation. We talked on the phone all the time, about the kids and about the company."

When it came time for John to make the decision of whose trusted hands he would leave the company in, he decided that it should be Cindy, as JR was still learning and growing for the time being. The decision to give Cindy the controlling interest in the company meant that she would run the Galardi Group, and whatever happened after he was gone would be up to her. It was a big responsibility, and not everyone in the company was comfortable with the idea. But Cindy was. She knew what she intended to do to carry on John's legacy, find new and creative ways to ensure the company's future, and protect it as a family-owned business. Cindy concludes, "At the end, John entrusted me with the most precious things he had: his children and his business." Cindy rose to the occasion to lead the company without hesitation.

One more major decision John needed to resolve was to name a co-trustee of his estate. John reserved that job for his eldest daughter, Teresa. He had always appreciated Teresa's analytic mind and her ability with numbers, which was so similar to his own way of thinking. Teresa had graduated from the University of Miami with a business degree, and John knew she could handle the assignment. He was right. Within two years of his passing, Teresa had successfully dealt with the complex legalities of John's personal financial holdings and resolved every issue with a cool and assured hand.

In December 2012, John was diagnosed with pancreatic cancer, putting an end to the speculation of what had been causing a variety of symptoms. JR dropped everything and moved to Newport Beach to be with his father, but it wouldn't take long for the cancer to do its work. On April 13, 2013, the family said goodbye to their beloved patriarch.

John Galardi was the embodiment of the American Dream:

a young man from a small town with a vision, fueled by a solid work ethic, an overwhelming urge to succeed, and a love of family. Not only did John go on to establish the largest hot dog chain in the world, but he also touched the lives of thousands. Just like that day back on Colorado Boulevard in 1958, the sun will always shine down on the memory of John Galardi as a good, honest, decent man.

Knowing that family was at the heart of John's vision, his family has continued the business with that same ethos. In their various roles within the company, JR, Cindy, Karen, and others have done what John Galardi would be most proud of: they have strengthened the Galardi Group and continue to build on their success without compromising any of John's core beliefs.

Since John's passing, Wienerschnitzel, Hamburger Stand, and Tastee-Freez sales continue to climb. With 330 stores in operation, the Wienerschnitzel management team is looking forward to reaching a goal of 500 stores.

That sounds like a plan that John Galardi would wholeheartedly endorse.

JR Galardi speaks with emotion as he relates this story—"My dad told me the proudest day of his life was the day he bought his dad, Ross Galardi, dinner for the first time. I never forgot that, and a week before my dad passed, I took him out and bought him dinner for the first time. On the drive home, he looked at me with tears in his eyes—which surprised me because I had never really seen him cry before—and told me that he was proud that I was his son. That moment replays in my head every day as the proudest day of my life."

"I would say that John was probably one of my best friends and taught me how to run a business. And when I say 'taught me how to run a business,' he taught me the small things, the day-to-day things. I learned that you can't micromanage people, which was something John did not do. When there was a problem, John would get right on it. He'd say, 'Okay, what's the problem, and why are we doing this about it?' I don't ever really remember John saying, 'Oh boy, we have some problems here.'"

- Dennis Tase
The former president of the Galardi Group

Hungry for profit

Wienerschnitzel owner John Galardi has built a fast-food empire

By Louisa Shepard
The Register

Wienerschnitzel 50th Anniversary
1961-2011

JOHN GALARDI, 1938 – 2013

Built hot dog restaurant into empire

BY STEVE CHAWKINS

W
hen John Galardi saw a man holding down the parking lot of a modest restaurant

out as he poured himself into the fast-food business. At 20, he worked double shifts managing three part-time jobs. With help from his parents, who borrowed on their furniture, he bought the restaurant for $12,000. Within a short time, he built his first Der Wienerschnitzel, in Los Angeles' Wilmington neighborhood.

He said he ate two or three hot dogs a day, seven days a week, for more than six years as the manager of his burgeoning operation.

He was among the first fast-food operators to set up a drive-through lane. The aim was to thin out the crowd of rowdy kids who were congregating at night in his parking lot.

"I'd walk out, and sometimes find 100 kids drunk and chase them off," he told the Orange County Business Journal in 1987. "I did a little survey and found out they were 100% of my problems and only 3% of my business."

By the time Galardi was 25, he was a millionaire. However, he expanded his business too quickly and borrowed too much — problems he spent years correcting.

"I followed the advice of Wall Street," he said. "I stopped making decisions and let other people do it. And I had to clean up the mess."

Galardi stepped back from daily management of his privately run company in 1991. In the meantime, he took a year off to ski in Aspen, Colo., and found for many years dividing his time between Aspen and Orange County.

A resident of Newport Beach, Galardi is survived by his wife, Jane, and four children.

steve.chawkins@latimes.com

DER WIENERSCHNITZEL

"We all have basically the same food, cooked in the same machines and sold by the same computers," he said. "It gets down to a corporate identification and a couple of meat items."

easy to make at home. He dressed up the hot dog and succeeded in providing a very crave-able product at very low prices.

Galardi, in a 1984 Times interview, was frank about trying to distinguish Wienerschnitzel from its competitors.

"In this industry, we all have basically the same food, cooked in the same machines and sold by the same computers," he said. "It gets down to a corporate identification and a couple of meat items."

Not to mention the chili, which in a 2012 commercial, he called "my secret weapon."

Born on March 4, 1938, in Kansas City, Mo., Galardi grew up in a small-town atmosphere "playing basketball, chasing girls and working," he told The Times. His father fixed appliances and his mother worked at Sears before moving, with Galardi and two of his brothers, to California.

Galardi briefly attended junior college in Pasadena but dropped

...maintain close con-
...and supervision of every phase of
their fast-growing franchise, operation,
while continuing to manage their owner-

DER WIENERSCHNITZEL BIRTHPLACE

AT THIS LOCATION JULY 3, 1961, THE FIRST OF DER WIENERSCHNITZELS NATIONWIDE CHAIN OPENED ITS DOORS

W Wienerschnitzel
HISTORIC LANDMARK

Hot dog chain is golden

June 10 2011   Register paper Orange County

Irvine-based Wienerschnitzel, the world's largest hot dog chain, hits the big 5-0 this year.

Not bad for a misnamed company in an era when about 29 percent of U.S. businesses survive 10 years, according to the Office of Advocacy in the U.S. Small Business Administration.

John Galardi, then 23, was itching to start his own restaurant after working four years for Glenn Bell, founder of Taco Bell.

JAN NORMAN
REGISTER WRITER

He decided on a hot dog stand on Pacific Coast Highway in Wilmington because "no one else was doing hot dogs," says Tom Amberger, current Wienerschnitzel vice president of marketing.

Bell's wife was looking through a cookbook and saw a recipe for Wiener Schnitzel, a Viennese version of breaded cutlet – which has nothing to do with sausages, hot dogs or sauerkraut – and suggested the name to Galardi.

"He thought it was the silliest thing he ever heard of, but it stuck," Amberger says.

The original name was Der Wienerschnitzel, but the company dropped the Der in 1978.

Early photos of Wienerschnitzel show that the restaurant sold hot dogs for 15 cents. It sold three versions: chili, mustard and kraut.

The company isn't going all the way back to 15-cent dogs in this golden anniversary year, but it will sell the original three for 61 cents on July 17, Amberger says.

Wienerschnitzel owes its growth to another concept that was on the rise in 1961: franchising. A company would come up with a brand, operating system and group marketing and get others to invest to "own their own business."

Today, Wienerschnitzel sells 120 million hot dogs a year from 351 units, some 90 percent of which are franchisees, in 10 states. The hot dog chain is also part of Galardi Group that includes The Hamburger Stand and Tastee Freez, which was a shared-location cross-branding effort with Wienerschnitzel.

50th ANNIVERSARY 1961-2011

Franchisees have played a big part in Wienerschnitzel's corporate culture, Amberger says. Some units, including ones in Brea and Buena Park, are testing the Hailey Special, chili cheese fries in a hot dog bun, created by a franchisee in Clovis, N.M.

"We'll see how it works out. If it does well, we'll roll it out company-wide," Amberger says.

One of the franchisees who has been around the longest is Paul Hironimus, who owns stores in Westminster, Lakewood, Norwalk and Whittier.

"I met John Galardi in 1959 when we started playing basketball together," Hironimus recalls. "He was always talking about getting into the restaurant business. He asked me to loan him $5,000. I didn't have it; I was a draftsman."

After Galardi started Wienerschnitzel, he hired Hironimus to be a supervisor in 1965. Thirteen years later Hironimus wanted to be a franchisee.

"Everybody ... business and ... tainly changed ... John. Once I ... hot dogs?' He sa ...

Somewhere a ... Bass, who had de ... ed Airlines and c ... red W with the c ...

Amberger thi ... the company na ... was supposed to ... mustard.

Galardi, 73, no ... 1970s and perma ... Orange County ... Dennis T ...

Wiener ... about it ... each mon ...hnitzel buys ... erage cu ...fez for an ... food, A ...ted sum, ... 500 carse cream ... all of its ...rants.

Wienerschnitzel awaken...

...usiness

hot dogs on the back burner

t-dog chain chills out

Top dog

FAST FOOD: After years of flat sales, the mustard is finally back on the Wienerschnitzel.

By GREG HARDESTY
The Orange County Register

NEWPORT BEACH — Still noshing after all these years.

"I took my two kids and a German boy staying with us to a Denver Nuggets (basketball) game the other day, and between us we had five hot dogs," says Colorado-resident John Galardi.

After 37 years, the Wienerschnitzel founder hasn't tired of the fare that made him rich.

Neither have consumers, who have made Wienerschnitzel the nation's largest hot-dog chain. The Newport Beach company plans to take the red-and-yellow A-frames international this year.

"If you want a hot dog, they're certainly the place to go," says Bob Sandelman, a Brea restaurant consultant.

After years of flat sales, the 295-unit chain is on a roll. Sales last year increased about 7 percent to $142 million, and the company has posted 15 consecutive months of record revenues. Privately held Wienerschnitzel doesn't release income figures.

But as Los Angeles Lakers broadcaster Chick Hearn would say, the mustard was almost off the hot dog four years ago.

Sales and profits were flagging. New menu items like hamburgers and chicken sandwiches were confusing customers bred on the chain's hot dog smothered in cheese, onions and chili.

stores last year and plans to open 19 more by July. Also on tap are the first outlets outside the United States, in Mexico and Guam.

Through it all has been Galardi. Seven years of bringing the company out of the woods in the early '70s took its toll. He divorced and took a five-year ...

The yellow, A-frame roof of original Wienerschnitzel restaurant... name that sounded vaguely Austrian but had nothing to do with...

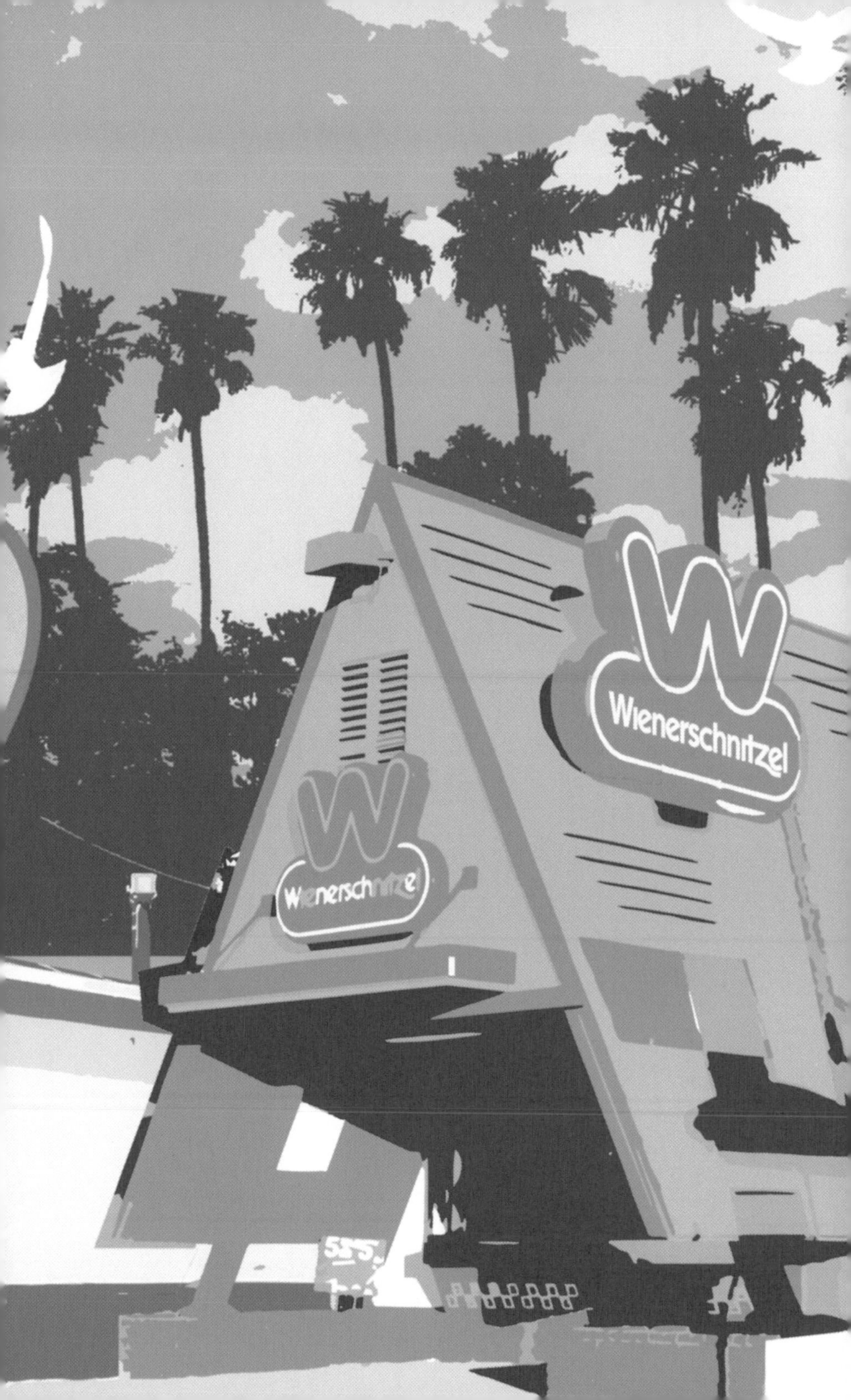

PART
TWO

Early Life and Dad

10

My name is JR Galardi, and my father is a legend.

In my life, I've had the privilege to be many things and live in many places—but at the core, I'm a Colorado kid. I was born in Long Beach, but I lived briefly on the Balboa Peninsula, then Newport Beach, and we moved to San Juan Capistrano, where I attended Saint Margaret's private school up until I turned six. Next was Aspen, Colorado, where we lived until I turned ten. I attended an international school for two years in France, then returned to Aspen, then went back to Newport Beach for a summer, and finally settled in Aspen one last time. I was even an exchange student in Japan for a couple months. Thus, I've been fortunate enough to see and experience a *lot* of the world before I was ever expected to head out into it on my own.

Regardless of my adventures, or how far or long we traveled, I always went back to California to work in my dad's company each summer. It was my choice, and I went there because I looked forward to the time spent at my dad's side. By the time I was born, his schedule was such that he and I were able to spend a lot of quality time together. With my two oldest sisters, he was always away on business, always out of the house, or sometimes even out of the country. Dad was still building the company back then, adding franchises and streamlining his process, so he wasn't around to be a father to his children. That's the harsh reality of the tough life of an entrepreneur, and when he was starting out, Dad was no exception. When I grew up, he had already developed the company to the size he wanted and was ready to retire. Although the dad I knew wasn't the same man my sisters knew, he worked to make sure he was present as much as possible with me.

When I use the term "quality time," I don't mean to say we were just under the same roof. Dad played with me, carried me around, sat by me at the dinner table for meals, and tucked me in at night. When my dad was with me, he was home. I saw his father side, but I didn't experience his business side until I was much older. He kept that part of himself hidden while I was young, and I will be forever thankful to him for that, even though it was such a large part of who he really was. In that, he allowed me to experience a unique side of him—a side that he wasn't able to give his other children—and it helped mold me into who I am today: the son of John Galardi, the son who took the reins of his business and whose mission it is to carry on that same legacy.

My memories of my childhood with my dad are vivid, and

that is due, largely in part, to the vivid nature of my father in general. When I was a kid, people I would meet would ask me, "What does your dad do? How does your family make a living?" and I would answer, "My dad started a restaurant chain called Wienerschnitzel. Have you heard of it?" Not everyone had, but those numbers dwindled over the years. As a kid, I began to realize I was part of something huge, and I had a front-row seat to the man who made it all happen.

One of my clearest recollections of seeing how others regarded my dad happened when I was eight years old and I accompanied him to Las Vegas at a Wienerschnitzel convention. While walking through a casino, we couldn't walk two steps without somebody stopping him to talk or snap a picture—these are not the exaggerations of a child's mind. I walked next to him in this kind of awed stupor, and it quickly dawned on me that my dad was someone special . . . not just, "I love you, Dad, you're great!" kind of special, but the special that other people recognize, gravitate toward, and want to emulate. The special that changes the world. I was stunned with how many people looked up to my father. I was one of them, of course, but he's my dad. I watched him grow as my perception of him gradually entered reality. This was John Galardi, founder of one of the most successful restaurant chains in the world.

And people looked up to him for a reason.

Over the time I spent with him throughout my childhood, adolescence, and early adulthood, I came to learn all the reasons why people looked up to him. Sure, he was a wealthy businessman, but he was so much more than that. He was an entrepreneur, an innovator. He was a job creator. Wienerschnitzel employed thousands of people at that time—across several states. Each Wienerschnitzel building held thirty workers, at least. There were the original restaurants, then the franchises, and the corporate office. It seemed like every day more and more people could go to work, make a living, and feed their families, all because my dad opened a hot dog stand. From a young age, that was something I could understand because I could see it for myself.

Dad furthered my understanding of what made others regard him as special by including me in more and more aspects of work over the years. As a kid, he took me to company events and meetings—opportunities for me to experience what it was all about without pushing it onto me or creating a sense of lingering obligation within me. Once, he brought me to a big stage production in Hawaii, set up by his company to launch the latest advertising campaign of new commercials. This was a big event for a kid. Posters, banners, balloons—the whole nine yards. At one point, I looked around and understood that it was all for him. I sat there taking in the cheers, the clapping, and the handshakes, and thought, *Geez, man. Who is this person?*

There, in front of me, was an aspect of my father that I'd never encountered. The man who tucked me in at night had suddenly transformed into a complete stranger to me. When it came to his work, he was a different person, almost like a split personality. When he got up on stage to speak, all the clamor ceased and you could hear a pin drop. As an adult, I've noticed I have a different demeanor when I'm on a company Zoom call than I have just hanging out with friends. I learned how to differentiate family man demeanor from businessman demeanor from a fairly young age, and now, I think my dad and I are alike in that way all thanks to how he raised me.

I had the best of both worlds with John Galardi at the fatherhood helm. He knew how to take his own interests and find ways to incorporate them into time with me. He'd gone to college on a basketball scholarship back in the day, so naturally, he loved the sport and wanted his son to love it, too. We used to play basketball together as a daily pastime. At our house on Balboa Peninsula, we had a little basketball hoop in our yard that backed up to the bay. There were countless times the tide would rise too high and our yard would flood and interrupt our game at some point, so we'd have to call it quits for the day. High water or not, he was always in control of when we left. Even against something as inevitable as the tide, he was the one who decided when enough was enough.

Dad wasn't a harsh man, at least not to me. Out of the two of them, my mother was more of the enforcer in the house, but she definitely played that "I'm going to tell your father" card, at which point I'd plead, "I'm so sorry, let's talk about this." He wasn't abusive in the least, and he almost never got mad, but the thought of him being mad, especially at me, was more than I could bear. I was terrified of disappointing him, of not being enough in his eyes. He kept me challenged and expected me to put forth an effort no matter the given task. I could make mistakes, which are always a part of progress, but he wanted to make sure I never messed up too badly. He taught me that the result isn't as important as the effort it takes to get there.

No matter how great of a parent you are, no child is perfect, and I was a dumb kid who did dumb things like everyone else. When I was fifteen, I was arrested for playing with a laser pointer at a hotel. My brother and I had this laser that reached for miles. We shone that stupid thing everywhere from the eighteenth floor of the hotel, at people, at cars, even a helicopter, which had a spotlight that went dark the instant we shone our laser at it. It turned out to be a police helicopter that was out looking for two troublemakers with a red light, and it was joined soon after by a second helicopter, then a big group of cop cars driving around. We thought it was hilarious, and we kept it up for maybe an hour before they apparently zeroed in on our building as the source. They were pretty close, but they thought it was the floor above us and raided the room of an older couple. It was the night before Thanksgiving and I tried to get my brother to go to bed, but he decided to take one more shot at the helicopter, which finally tipped the cops off to our exact location. They came and banged on the door, and there I was in my boxers with a hallway full of hotel security and law enforcement. They came in with guns drawn and cuffed us, stuck us in the hallway, and then completely destroyed our room. It didn't take long for them to find the laser pointer and arrest us both. Eric, my brother, was eighteen and old enough to be taken to jail.

They called our parents and my dad answered.

"I'm not getting up. They're idiots. Take them to jail."

Dad had already been through teenage rebellion with my sisters years before, so this was nothing new to him. My mom, however, went alone to the station and got me released into her parental custody with a charge of terrorism—which is a felony. My brother went to jail, and the next morning, my mom promptly bailed him out on the way to Thanksgiving brunch with my grandmother. I was tasked with bringing him extra clothes so he could change into Thanksgiving brunch appropriate attire in the car. We were sworn to secrecy and specifically told not to tell my grandma that her grandsons were terrorists. We made it through the meal in one piece, but we all had to put on one hell of an "Everything's fine!" show for Grandma.

The next day, Dad had his sit-down with us in our room.

"You guys are idiots. I might have done the same thing at your age, but not for two damn hours. You made it on CNN. They ran a story about your idiocy."

At the time, I couldn't believe that something so small had caused so much trouble, so it became a valuable life lesson for me about the reality of the repercussions of my actions. We went to court and managed to get the charges knocked down; I got off because I was a minor, and the judge gave Eric community service . . . not too bad for child terrorist felons.

My mom wanted to crack our skulls. She threatened to send us to boarding school. She yelled and stamped her feet and told us we were on thin ice—but not Dad. He let the consequences of our actions, and the notoriety they brought, teach the lesson for him.

And then he let us move on.

Neither one of my parents was better than the other; they each filled the role they needed to. One of them had to be the stricter parent, leaving room for one of them to take on the more level-headed role; that's how partnerships work. The methods my mom employed kept us aligned to the day-to-day expectations of how we should behave as children, which children absolutely need.

There are certain aspects of parenting that can only be recognized for their great job after the fact, when you're able to look back and reflect on what made a difference, what worked so well for you, in retrospect. Dad talked to us like adults, and that made a long-term impact. He didn't punish us, yell at us, or ground us to our rooms for a month like some parents might. He didn't allow his anger to rule his intention, which was to raise sons who could think for themselves. His methods aligned us to who we would become, and he hoped we would become more than himself.

Several years later, as an adult in college, I had an opportunity to put Dad's methods to the test. I was working for a modeling agency and decided to leave because checks started bouncing and everything was coming apart. I'd done a show with a woman I later ran into at a party, and we got to talking about how the agency had failed and we'd been forced to look for that next thing.

At one point in our conversation, she looked at me and asked me point blank, "Do you want to come help me with my new business?"

I accepted right away.

Her company, Souls in Action Entertainment, which had been in business for about a year, promoted concerts, and I set right to work. We looked into artist management and decided to expand in that direction. This was in Denver, where all the big venues were owned by AEG or Live Nation. The biggest venue, Red Rocks, was owned by the state. So we started renting venues for performances and got a lot of new and big-name deejays from around the world with huge cult followings. Dubstep was big at the time and we almost exclusively handled EDM. It got to the point where I'd heard so much EDM that I couldn't listen to it anymore, and still can't to this day. But we backfilled the opening slots at each concert with these artists and tried to help the bigger companies sell out on tickets. After a while, we became extremely efficient at selling out the smaller venues and, eventually, the huge venues too.

Sometimes we'd get a flat rate and sometimes we'd get a percentage of the door sales, but I always tried to negotiate for more. I learned in school that Jimmy Buffet was the only musician ever to get a combination of a flat rate, a percentage of the door sales, and a percentage of the bar, thanks to his song "Margaritaville." He convinced everyone that the song influenced drink sales due to people craving margaritas every time he sang it, and it worked for him—didn't work for me, but I still tried all the time because it was worth a shot.

During my time in that position, I never wanted to use a penny of my dad's money for any of the work I was doing and made it a point not to. I wanted to be successful in my own right, without anything I perceived as a "handout" at the time. So, any time I got in a financial bind, I figured out how to funnel some of my work savings into covering costs in tight spots, but that didn't always work. There was one particular instance where I felt well and truly cornered. I hired a deejay and owed him eight hundred dollars, and no matter how I tried to move cash around, I just couldn't pay him on time. So I went to my mom and asked for the money to cover the deejay, which she gave me right away. I used it to pay the man and paid my mom back in full after our next show. That was the only time I got stuck and had to rely on my parents. I knew I could have put the deejay on hold and delayed his payment, but ultimately, paying the vendor I hired on time was much more important than any pride I lost in asking a parent for help. That experience helped me maintain the integrity of my business, and that's all that really mattered.

Grit and determination were ingrained into me on a fundamental level simply by knowing what it took my dad to start something from nothing and grow it to an empire. It didn't have to be said to me; it wasn't a lesson that was drilled into me. Instead, grit and determination manifested naturally in the energy I was putting into weekly shows—four shows a week on Mondays, Wednesdays, Fridays, and Saturdays. I still had classes Tuesdays and Thursdays at 8 a.m., so I would run home, take a shower, pop an Adderall, and chug a Red Bull before heading off to class, day after day after day.

The entirety of my whirlwind learning experience occurred while I was still in college. When I graduated in 2012, the world would open up even more, but as we continuously sold out left and right, developing relationships with everyone from sound techs to CEOs of music companies, I soon realized that Denver was a small pond. Although it had a sizeable music scene, it had one glaring issue that couldn't be overlooked—no matter how successful we were, we'd never own the venues. We would always be stuck dumping money into rent, and it added up. The business would cap out if we didn't adapt.

We had to shift out of stagnancy, so I determined that a move to LA would be the most beneficial. We did some shows in LA and San Diego, but then I got distracted with one of the underground hip hop acts called TiRon and Ayomari. I hosted some concerts for them, and we just got along really well. They were in need of a tour manager, and I accepted. It may not have been the best decision, but I wanted a change of lifestyle and it sounded like too good of a time to pass up. We worked together for about six months, two of which we were on the road, driving around in a minivan and sleeping on wood floors in Brooklyn. It was fun for a while, but I woke up one morning, hungover and sore, and looked around myself in sort of a daze. I happened to be at just the right angle to see under the apartment's stove, and there, the thousand-yard death stare of a dead rat met my eyes.

That moment—from how my body felt, how the air around me smelled, to the glazed eyes of the deceased rodent—acted as a wakeup call. These artists partied and stayed out all night, and they wanted me to join in . . . but they were able to sleep late and not worry about a thing until the next concert. I couldn't. I had business to attend to. I was supposed to be in charge; I had to manage their venues and scheduling and contacts, make sure they got up on time, make sure they had everything they needed for the day, make sure they were fed . . . and then it hit me—I was living someone else's life, plain and simple.

I came to the conclusion that you can love the people around you, but their reality isn't always aligned with your reality, and you can't let them overtake your reality with theirs. I loved these people, but there I was, drained of life, sprawled out on the floor next to a dead rat. I could feel my skin crawl, and whether it was due to hangover anxiety or dehydration, I had this realization that I was on the wrong path. I forced myself up on unsteady legs and staggered to the shower. As I readied myself for the day and woke up externally, I felt myself awaken internally. Somehow, that dead rat was symbolic of my current future. Despite being profitable, my lifestyle wasn't sustainable. I saw very clearly that I was headed on a road straight to burnout, and in order to avoid it, I had to make some big changes. Just as Dad had hoped would happen, I felt like I was meant for something better.

From that moment forward, there was an encompassing energy within me that, if I tried to articulate into words, simply translated to an inner voice reminding me that it was time to get to work: we were in the middle of a tour, and I still had a job to do. Over the next two weeks, I followed that energy's lead and put everything I had left in the tank into my role, still partying with them, but running on fumes. I eventually battened down the hatches and really focused on my responsibilities for the first time, and I ended up having a fantastic experience just being in charge. I knew this chapter of my life was coming to a close, so I gave it my all because I knew I wouldn't be back.

I credit my renewed invigoration for life after my dead rat experience directly to my father's influence. My father is a legend because of his indomitable entrepreneurial spirit. He loved the business of business his entire life. He was a student of customers, and although his empire was built from a hot dog stand, his contribution to the world is one that I am honored to carry on. My father raised me to come to understand business naturally, not forcibly. I've known so many successful parents with children who don't amount to anything in their lives, who squander their gifts and don't do a damn thing to help others. I don't know if the entrepreneurial trait is genetic or not, but I'm so grateful that my father taught me, in his subtle and patient way, his work ethic and his drive to do more—to be more.

I came across two short quotes that really exemplify how I was raised, and I'd like to share them here:

"I have found the best way to give advice to your children is to find out what they want and then advise them to do it." —Harry S. Truman

"If you want children to keep their feet on the ground, put some responsibility on their shoulders." —Abigail Van Buren (*Dear Abby*)

When the time comes for me to have children of my own, I want to instill in them the same principles that I was taught. Just like my dad, I want my kids to be better than I am, to appreciate what they have, and to think clearly for themselves no matter what course they choose through life.

JR and Skylar handing out candy to kids in a remote village in India, 1999.

Cindy and John with their son, JR, before his senior prom.

Earning My Way

11

"If you go to time out, I'll give you a quarter."

Bribery. It's terrible, but it worked like a charm. I happily ran to time out and took my punishment because, when it was over, I had another coin for the piggy bank. As long as I had my own money, I had freedom. Any time I got into trouble when I was really young, my mom would put forth her best efforts to send me to time out, but I always refused to go. I'd just sit there, stubborn and defiant, which only served to further frustrate her. But one day, she figured it out.

Mom also paid me to read. We started with twenty-five cents per page, which was awesome for books like *Green Eggs and Ham,* but I quickly gamed the system and jumped to longer titles like *Harry Potter*—so we had to start haggling over the price of finishing books. There are probably loads of child psychologists and parenting specialists who have a million reasons why you shouldn't pay your kids to read, but maybe they're missing the point. I can vouch for my mom that it worked. I learned to absolutely love reading because there was an immediate payout for it, but there was also a long-term investment in it.

The average kid doesn't voluntarily want to sit and read; they want to run around outside, play in the mud, and hit each other with sticks. But, as in most cases in life, sometimes we must do things we'd rather not, and it helps to know that effort brings reward. For the cost of a handful of quarters, Mom's foresight established a lifelong habit in me. All that really matters is she found a way to get her boy to read, and that's what she taught me: whatever works, as long as it works.

I've been accustomed to earning my way ever since I can remember. When I was six years old, I got a job selling newspapers. My mom would drive me to the local paper, the *Aspen Times*, and they'd give me stacks of newspapers. I'd go sell them on the street for twenty-five cents apiece, and I'd just walk around town all day like some Dickens character. My mom was thrilled, because she could just drop me off and go about her day while I got busy with my job. You might recoil from reading that today, but it worked for us. I loved it.

After some trial and error, I figured out the best way to sell papers was to go into bars during happy hour. I learned that drunk people tended to be fairly liberal with their money, and I'd just walk in with my vest packed full of newspapers. Rather than quarters, they gave me a dollar, or five dollars, or even ten sometimes. Taking advantage? Maybe, but remember that I was six. They were just really shocked to see a little kid out with a side hustle, and I think the surprise of it made an impact on them. I'd walk out of the bar with my pockets stuffed with cash instead of newspapers. It felt phenomenal.

Other odd jobs followed, like fence painting. We had a big property and my parents hired me to go out and sand, repair, and repaint all the fencing around the house. This assignment was part of my allowance, you could say. It wasn't easy work, and I did a lot of sweating in the sun to get things done, but it felt good to look back at the line of fence and see what I'd accomplished. I was maybe nine years old, but I did the job well. After a while, one of our neighbors came over and offered me a hundred bucks to do his fence next. To a nine-year-old, a cool hundred is all the money in the world. The work was always over too soon; I wanted a more permanent method of income, but I'd have to wait.

I saved every penny I earned; they belonged to me and I didn't spend one of them. Some might view that as greed, but it's not the same thing. It wasn't so much having the money that I craved, but the method of acquiring it. My work equaled ownership, and that was exciting. Something inside told me not to spend it, and that inner voice was really strong. It got to the point that if my parents gave me money for school lunch, I'd just pocket the cash and sit in the cafeteria, waiting until everyone else finished eating so I could eat their leftovers. I was obsessed.

Dad caught on to my scrimping and took the opportunity to negotiate a deal with me. We agreed that whatever money I could save by the time I was sixteen, he would match in a car purchase. And I wanted that car so badly, I'd do anything to get it. It didn't matter what kind of car; I just knew I wanted a "nice" one. I wanted my reward to be significant, not just the first thing that came past or the cheapest deal. Dad knew an elderly woman who couldn't drive anymore, and she had a 1999 Audi A6 with three thousand miles on it. She explained she wanted to get it out of her garage, so I cleaned out my bank account and paid her a visit. I put $8,000 in her hands—Dad, good on his word, covered another $8,000 himself—and walked out the door with the first "big" purchase I'd ever made.

I had to stare at that car in the driveway for four long months before I could drive, and you can bet that was excruciating for a teenager wanting to run a little wild.

Turning sixteen solved all my problems. Not only did I have a dream car, but I finally qualified for a work permit, which meant no more odd jobs for pocket change. I could submit applications and reel in paychecks to refill my empty savings account and hopefully cover my gas expense. My first "real" job was at a board shop that sold and serviced snowboards and skateboards. They didn't offer a big selection, so it was easy for me to pick up how to restock inventory and do sales for their products, and it got me interested in how to use the boards in my personal time. The pay was okay, but I decided to take on a second job scooping ice cream at a Ben & Jerry's, because more work meant more money. I filled so many cones that my wrists hurt from all the scooping, but I couldn't wrap my brain around memorizing the menu. They expected all their workers to know every ingredient and flavor and be able to recall them on demand, and I just couldn't do it. I cheated and looked at the huge menu board next to the cash register every time, and after a while, I just felt like the job wasn't for me anymore.

My mom, who went to the gym a few times a week—she still does, well into her seventies—found out one of her workout buddies had two young boys that needed to be looked after, so I was offered a job looking after the boys as their "manny." I was seventeen or eighteen at the time, trying to save up some money before going to college, and the job sounded perfect. I would arrive at 6 a.m. to hang out with these kids and keep them fed and busy until 3 or 4 p.m., then took them to whatever sports practice they had that day. I had zero experience, but I figured everything would be fine as long as they didn't die. It worked out so well because they were just two little boys who looked up to me; they wanted to do whatever I wanted to do. I could take them skateboarding, or to float the river, or even just hang out with my friends, and they loved every minute of it. And neither of them died, so that's a plus.

I had gotten into a groove—I had work, and in high school, I joined the Aspen freestyle competitive snowboarding team. Every Monday, Wednesday, and Friday, I got out of school around lunch time and headed to the hill for practice. My heavy training schedule proved awesome for competition, but it also meant I had to make up the credits by going to junior college at night. I gave it everything I had and ended up taking so many junior college classes that I was on track to finish high school in three and a half years as a seventeen-year-old. The plan was to graduate in December and dive into some international snowboarding competitions, where amateurs and pros competed against each other, before college. I was well on my way.

Then I hit a snag.

In November of my senior year, I went to a house party, and while I was having a great time, I got drunk. Everyone was doing their thing, listening to music, dancing, or making out—whatever seemed fun. All in all, it was a standard high school party.

At one point, one of my friends came into the room and said, "Who wants to box in the garage?"

No one took him up right away, so I stepped up.

"That sounds super fun! Let's do it!"

Now, I didn't hit my growth spurt until nineteen, so I was maybe 5'6" and a hundred and twenty pounds soaking wet. I was not a big kid at all. When we got to the garage and squared off in a ring of teenagers, I realized this guy was twice my size and maybe even drunker than I was.

But no biggie, right? It was all just for fun.

There were no gloves, so we agreed to bare-knuckle box. In my mind, this meant going half-speed and sort of slapping with a closed hand, like friends do sometimes. We set our stances and bumped fists like they did in the pros, and I got ready for a friendly bout as our classmates cheered and whooped.

And that's when my opponent stepped forward and hit me as hard as he could with a right hook, breaking my skull just above my left ear. There was no bobbing or weaving, no shadow box throws. There was only immediate pain, which exploded throughout my body as I simultaneously lost my balance. As I spun and fell from that first hit, he lunged and unloaded another punch into the back of my head, breaking the bone there as well. I hit the ground and blacked out.

People told me later that I jumped up immediately and said, "I'm done. That hurt. Good fight," and then gave the guy a hug before walking out of the garage to head back to the party. Still outside of my memory, friends said I went and got some ice cream, took some Advil because my head hurt, and someone gave me a shot of alcohol to dull the pain. I came "back online" at some point during the night, but I couldn't really take stock of the situation because I was so drunk from doing more shots.

But I felt tired. I found some stairs that led to the basement and saw a couch, which seemed like a godsend. I just wanted to sleep things off, so that's what I did. My mind didn't wake back up, but I was told (again, after the fact) that I started yelling and screaming down in that basement and scared the hell out of everyone. Of course, this was a party with underage drinking, so no one wanted to call the police or notify anyone's parents because then we'd all be busted.

My shouting fit continued until someone finally called my mom to come get me. So, at 3:30 in the morning, my mom got out of bed and drove the half hour to where I was. She came downstairs to my couch and gave me the once-over. As far as she could tell, I was just drunk, so she started in with the usual, "You idiot. What do you think you're doing?" Then she realized that something was wrong. Really wrong.

Mom called 911 and tried to wake me up until an ambulance arrived to take me to the hospital. At the time, the hospital was very small and under-equipped to do much more than a quick X-ray, but the results showed that I had internal bleeding in my brain and swelling in my cerebellum.

They immediately called a Life Flight helicopter and loaded me on board, but they told my mom she couldn't come with me because I wouldn't survive the flight. When the brain incurs injury to the degree of internal bleeding and swelling, pressure builds and builds with nowhere to go until it collapses down your spine and you die. That typically happens if the victim doesn't get into surgery within six hours of the initial injury. It had already been well over six hours.

Mom wasn't having it. She was out of her mind with fear for her son's life, and she took a stand. She told the EMTs there was no way she would let that helicopter leave without her. Rather than fight with her, they let her board . . . with the understanding that these would be her last moments with me.

I made it through the flight and we landed at the new hospital, where the doctors immediately induced a coma. Six hours with a brain injury was enough to kill most people; I didn't get into surgery until nine hours after my K.O. While I was under the knife, they told my mom, "There's a lot of brain damage. If he dies, it will be because of all the swelling. His chances of survival are almost nothing. Even if he somehow survives the surgery, the damage is so extensive that he'll never be the same again. You'll have to take care of him for the rest of his life, however short it will be." The doctors said I had a 99.9% likelihood of dying.

I can't imagine what it was like for her to hear those words, or how she was able to keep from losing herself to despair, but thanks to some phenomenal medical professionals, I somehow came through the surgery intact. I was still in an induced coma, however, and it took a few days to come out of that.

When I awoke, my mind wasn't the same. I'd forgotten how to read and write, how to do math, and a dozen other basic skills that I'd always taken for granted. I felt like I knew the information in front of me, but when I tried to use my knowledge, nothing made sense. My brain was scrambled.

As I worked on the recovery process and relearning some things, I was able to sit up and move around a bit in bed. That felt promising, and all I could think about was getting out of that hospital. I wanted to go snowboarding again, and to hang out with my friends. A flash of realization hit me one day—I was supposed to go on a helicopter trip with my dad to snowboard in Alaska in a couple weeks. From that moment forward, the helicopter trip was all I could think about. I started to get a little better, but they told me there was a 99.9% chance (those same odds again) that I would need aftercare for the rest of my life. I thought to myself, *The hell I will,* and focused twice as hard on recovery.

And then I discovered I couldn't walk.

The temptation to get stuck on what I had lost was powerful, but I took it all as a challenge. I could do this. I could beat this.

Call it willpower or grit or whatever you like, but I learned how to walk again in less than two weeks. After being told such insurmountable odds, I thought that was pretty good.

I had some intense physical therapy for another two weeks. My first goal was just to take one step while two people held me up. The next was to make it to the chair by the wall while three people held me up. Then across the room, down the hall, and so forth. Once I got the motion of walking down, my goal became doing it with only two people assisting me, then down to one person, until I could walk on my own using the wall as balance. Finally, I was able to walk unassisted once more. I had done so well that they decided to let me try going home, but I had a relapse and regressed with really severe headaches. I couldn't stand to be in any sort of light without almost passing out from the pain, so back to the hospital I went for another two weeks while they monitored my brain for swelling and bleeding. I don't remember much about my second stint in the hospital, truth be told.

I made it through, but none of the medical professionals working with me could figure out why. Brain injury victims with half of the damage I incurred went into vegetative states and needed serious care every moment of the day, unable to feed themselves or even wipe their asses. So why was I okay?

I got a call from the National Institute of Health, and they explained they were doing studies on traumatic brain injuries. They offered to pay me in return for coming to their facility so they could study my brain. My injuries had messed with a lot of my faculties, but I apparently still had the drive to earn money, so I accepted.

The NIH itself was gorgeous. "Facility" just didn't do it justice: it was more like a resort, with courtyards full of greenery and fountains. I felt at ease there, but I also had some hard work to do. For three hours, I went into the CAT scan machine and had to hold absolutely still while they took images of my brain. You have to lie on a super uncomfortable metal tray the entire time, and you can't move a muscle during that time, or else they have to restart everything. I didn't have much patience for it overall, so I eventually stopped going.

I've still never heard a word about what the CAT scan revealed. I wish they would have shared their findings with me, but I suppose that time has passed. The general hypothesis, at least on my end, of why I survived is that because my skull was fractured in two places, the swelling actually had room to expand somewhat further without building to lethal pressure. Turns out that second punch might have just saved my life.

My full recovery took a long time. I was seventeen and still had aspirations of going to snowboarding competitions all over the world, but I couldn't do any of that. All I could do was sit there and play *Guitar Hero* for six months while all my friends went to class and had fun. That sounds a little whiny, but I guess I did learn how to play a mean fake guitar. Not bad for a kid with brain damage and a 0.1% survival rate.

In the meantime, something had been happening in the background of my life. When I first came out of my coma, there was a police officer present in the room. He had originally been sent from Aspen to do an autopsy report on me because they assumed I was going to die on the helicopter. Once the brain swelling was in check and the doctors cleared me for visitation, the officer came to the side of my bed and asked, "Do you want to press charges against Robbie?"

"For what?" I replied.

"Assault and battery," said the cop.

"That's ridiculous," I told him. "We agreed to box together. It's not like he jumped me in an alley. We were drunk and it escalated too quickly for either of us to realize what was going on. Of course I don't want to press charges."

"Well," he said, "unfortunately, in Colorado, we have a lot of husbands who beat their wives, but the wives don't want to press charges because it could lead to further abuse. So there's something called the Battered Wife Law that means the state can press charges on behalf of someone if they feel it's justified, regardless of their consent."

That was exactly what happened. My friend, Robbie, the kid twice my size, got taken to court by the state and lost. I visited him in jail and we did the knuckles on the glass thing because I wanted to show him there were no hard feelings on my end. I didn't want him to be charged, but it was out of my control. He understood that he messed up, but it wasn't all his fault. When he got out of his stint behind bars, we went and got pizza and watched movies together.

We see each other all the time now.

***

My dad never wanted me to be idle. He'd tell me, "You've got to get your shit together. You've got to work. You can't lay around." I have to credit at least some of my intrinsic motivation to kick recovery's ass to his caution against idleness. He taught me that relaxation should be earned, at least for men. With my sisters, he just didn't engage in that mentality, but with me, he wanted to instill a sense that I should always strive to do more and be more. And he was old-school, so he felt that it was a man's responsibility to take care of the women in his life, to work hard so they didn't have to. A generation later, I still want to get off the couch to earn my way, and to take care of the people around me (not just the women), and I have him to thank for that.

Intolerance of idleness was about the extent of his mentoring for business in my early years. He didn't allow me into that aspect of his world until much later. We'd chat about sports and girls, and all the typical father/son things, but never his actual day-to-day work at the company. If he did mention business, it was always in very subtle ways. For instance, we'd be out for lunch and I'd order a soda and, while I enjoyed my beverage, Dad would tell me the profit margin on sodas. He'd say, "Did you know that one soda only costs ten cents, but we just paid a dollar-fifty for it?" I had no concept of that before he said it, but then he pointed around the restaurant at each one of the drinks and said, "Dollar-forty there, dollar-forty there, dollar-forty there." He was driving home the point that something so common had huge potential for profit. All that change was going into someone's pocket, and I wanted it.

Dad knew the art of subtlety. He knew he had to be subtle like this because, when it came down to it, I just wanted to go play. I wanted to ride my skateboard and run around chasing girls, so he knew to go slowly as he introduced various business concepts into my everyday life. He was so patient, and I never once felt like he was forcing me to follow in his footsteps. As I got older, around thirteen or so, he took me to work in the Newport Beach Wienerschnitzel for the first time. I put on the shirt and the name tag and just tried my best not to mess up.

My presence confused everyone. "You're the son of *the* John Galardi? The owner?" They wanted to take pictures with me, which was beyond strange to me at thirteen but makes sense in retrospect—my presence was unusual! Other employees were all polite and curious, and it seemed like everyone had a story to share about my dad, but the underlying, unspoken sentiment on everybody's mind seemed to be: "You're rich. You're the owner's son. Why are you working?"

It was important to me to show through my actions that I wasn't there to "play work"; I was serious. So, my first position at Wienerschnitzel began as a janitor. I cleaned the place top to bottom: dining room, entries, counters, and bathrooms. I scrubbed toilets and mopped up spills. They trained me at the same time, and I moved from janitorial to bagging food, which is the next step up. While I bagged, I learned how to use the fryer, then the hot dog grill, then on to hamburgers, the cash register, and finally the drive-thru—all the fundamental day-to-day, front-line worker knowledge. By the end of that summer, I could work any position in the restaurant. And, just like with the newspapers, I loved it.

The restaurant I worked at was something of a testing facility for new possibilities at Wienerschnitzel, and we wanted to see how beer would sell. We had a Budweiser tap and there I was, thirteen years old, pouring beer for customers. It didn't last long, but it was popular for a while. One day, I was pouring beers and these two police officers came in, dressed in their full uniforms, and ordered two 16-ounce beers.

I poured the drinks and handed them over, but one of the cops said, "You know, it's illegal for you to be pouring beer at your age."

"Isn't it illegal for you to be drinking on the job like this?" I replied.

I was a smartass, but they didn't know what to say and just went to their table without another word.

Dad used me for information about the company, just like he did with everyone else. There was nothing malicious or insensitive about it; it's just how he processed information and created new possibilities, and he never really took a break from it. We'd sit down at the end of my workday and he'd launch into a series of questions about how my shift went, what went smoothly and what didn't, and if I thought any improvements could be made. He was always on the lookout for opportunities to fine tune the business. Sometimes our lunch rush was so big that we'd have a line out the front door, so I'd tell him about it and he'd respond with something like, "What do you think about that? What's the cause?" He explained that each one of those customers standing in line represented royalty contributions to our way of life, and he'd break down the math for me. "If this person spends X amount of dollars, this percentage goes to the business, this percentage to overhead, and this percentage to profit." Each transaction at the cash register, every hot dog and soda, sent a slice to our family. It was mind boggling to think about all those slices coming from all those people in all those restaurants, day in and day out. Even as a young teen, I could hear the *cha-chings* echoing in from around the country.

When I wasn't working in the restaurant, I was traveling. Traveling was one of the cornerstones of my parents' belief in raising us: education through experience—which meant getting out there and seeing new things and meeting new people—was a far better pontificator than any lecturer in a classroom. So we traveled a ton. They set up special programs through my US schools so that I could move forward with my education without being penalized for going abroad. The international school in Nice, France, was an important part of that process. My expectation was to travel, journal about what I saw and did, then return with extensive reports for the whole class about where I'd been.

One of my most prolific experiences, and one from which I grew tremendously, was in India. When, at ten years old, you're sitting in a car and hear a knock on the window, only to look out and see someone your own age with one arm and one eye, holding a baby and begging for money, you are forced to grow and learn in that moment. I learned that it's a common practice for some people to take children from their families, mutilate them to garner pity, hand them a baby that belongs to someone else, and put them on the streets to beg. My mom's heritage is Indian, and she taught me to give the kids candy rather than money, because the money would always be taken away from them, but they got to keep the candy. We didn't want to reward or incentivize the mutilation practice, so we took loads of candy to India and the children would just lose their minds over it, because it was a kindness they almost never experienced.

On another trip to India, we went to the celebration of Holi. It goes by a lot of names in English, like Festival of Love or Festival of Spring, but the one you might recognize is Festival of Colors. It's one of their biggest holidays. Everyone in the country parties: marching bands, music, and dancing in the streets, and the ubiquitous bright colors of red, blue, yellow, and green, all denoting a different aspect of the Hindu beliefs. In honor of Krishna, who painted his face all colors to express his love for Radha, people throw colored powder on each other to celebrate happiness and love for one another.

So there I was, ten years old, watching all of this from a balcony above the street, and it blew my mind.

"Can I go down there?" I asked my mom.

"Go ahead," she said. "Just don't go far."

I didn't listen to anything past the "go ahead" and found myself on the street a moment later, surrounded by colors and smiling faces. I made friends with an Indian boy without either of us speaking a word of each other's language. It didn't matter that we came from different backgrounds, or how much our parents earned, or that our skin didn't match. When you're a kid, you know that everyone's the same; we all just want to be happy and have fun together. We hopped on his bike (I stood on the back pegs), and he handed me a Super Soaker full of colored water. To a chorus of cheers, we rode through the crowds as I blasted everyone with color, amazed at the pure happiness of everyone around me. Even the people in full suits headed to work got hit with powder and water, and only laughed and smiled all the more.

This type of education isn't something you're going to get sitting in a classroom. That's not to say traditional school is lacking merit, only that it's lacking this additional sense of humanity. I saw firsthand what goes on inside third-world countries, and no textbook can fully depict that. So many of us are unbelievably lucky to live where we do. I call it the "sperm lottery." No one gets to choose where they're born; they have to make the best of whatever situation they're handed, and it's not easy. If you're given a garbage roll of the dice, your chances of being successful are next to nothing, which is why it's so crucial for those with success to help others through philanthropy.

I grew up in a bubble. By that I mean, due to the places I lived, like Aspen or California, I didn't have a realistic worldview. What I saw walking around in these places was not indicative of how most of the world lived their lives. Skateboarding to the mall to hang out with my friends, catch a movie, and grab a pizza are all fun things, but they narrow one's perception of what's really happening outside the bubble. Socialization is important, but I can't stress enough how much traveling changed my life for the better. It popped the bubble.

Traveling as much as I did with my parents served as a motivator upon returning stateside; I always came home ready to earn my way. At seventeen, I interned at Wienerschnitzel's advertising agency and learned the marketing aspects of the company, which surprised me with their depth. The next year, I worked as a franchise area director overseeing thirty restaurants. I was one of the corporate field people who managed problems on a wide scale, putting out fires and ensuring each restaurant was working properly. It was a huge jump in responsibility, but it just felt right to me.

Before graduating from college, I made sure I gained experience working in a different environment than anything else I was accustomed to; I didn't work at Wienerschnitzel. I worked at a hedge fund company named UBS. I wanted to prove to myself that I was capable of transferring my successes thus far into a different, complex industry. I hated every moment there, but I also learned an important lesson: just because a job pays well doesn't mean it's a good fit—a lesson often overlooked when considering how you're going to invest the entirety of your life upon choosing a career. I learned the intangible value of the importance of pursuing careers that speak to us, and not settle for the first big paycheck that comes along.

After my brief stint in the music industry in 2012, I recognized a sense of time and how it wasn't slowing down. Dad was getting older. He didn't know he was sick at the time, but he wanted to pass on his legacy and wasn't sure I'd be a good fit to take his place. On my end, I didn't exactly relish the idea of working in hot dogs for the rest of my life. This was my dad's business; not mine. I wanted to build my own future, and I thought the key to that future was outside of Wienerschnitzel.

We agreed on a trial period. Twice a week, I'd drive to Newport, and twice a week, Dad would line up work meetings to fill the days. He told me, "I want you to come with me. You don't have to do anything; just be there to absorb and observe how I look at things and make my decisions." He wanted me to learn his mindset as sort of a last-ditch effort in case something happened to him—which turned out to be a pretty wise move.

"You don't need to have all the knowledge in the world," he said. "You just need to understand critical thinking and when to react— or not react—to the situation. You can learn all the marketing, operations, and accounting you want, but the one thing you won't be able to learn when I'm gone is how I look at the big picture."

Since he wasn't handling the day-to-day business, he was able to coordinate all his work affairs with the days I was present, and I followed him around, shadowing his actions. He had other ventures, like owning some apartment buildings and a gas station, but the lion's share of his time went to Wienerschnitzel. And I saw everything. I attended his every meeting, watched every negotiation, saw every handshake, mediation, and signature—

week after week. After all this time, I finally got to see the legend in his element, and it was awe-inspiring to experience this professional facet of the man I thought I knew so well as a father.

Outside of work, it was difficult for me to reconcile who he was with who I'd known. How had he kept this part of himself hidden from me for so long? Looking back now, I see that he wanted me to be free to choose my destiny, but at the time, he was an enigma. We'd go back home and have dinner, and he'd pull that veil back over himself; he was just Dad again. We'd chat about business (in general, not his work), money, girls, and sports, just as usual, but the tone had changed. I'd seen his other side—the corporate titan—and things felt so different now. It wasn't just the age gap between us (he was fifty years old when he had me), but a larger silence that could only be filled with truth.

JR, age 13, working at Wienerschnitzel

Passing the Torch

12

One of the biggest truths we come to as we grow into adulthood is the realization that our parents aren't perfect. I think all children go through this rite of passage at some point, but mine took a particularly long time because they hid things so well. And, honestly, I was sufficiently distracted with living my life that I didn't really stop to consider there might be more going on under the surface with them. They had their struggles, but I never once saw them fight or argue. That all happened behind closed doors and out of my presence, but it did happen.

I had memories of seeing couples fight on television, and I'd even seen my friends' parents get heated from time to time, but never Mom and Dad. I asked my mom once, "Don't you guys ever fight?"

She laughed and replied, "All the time, dear. We just don't do it in front of you."

They had both been divorced once before marrying, and they divorced each other when I was eighteen (after twenty-seven years together), so the whole "sanctity of marriage" thing never quite stood the test of time in my eyes, but Dad always treated her with utmost respect. My mom came from a very abusive home where screaming, throwing things, and physical aggression were all the norm, and my dad came from extreme poverty and rough living conditions, so one might assume they'd perpetuate their cycles with me and my siblings. Nothing could be further from the truth. Sure, they'd have little disagreements here and there:

"The soup's too hot, honey."

"No, it's fine. Just eat it."

But that was it. When it came to my dad, he knew when to let an argument die. And he carried that knowledge over from the living room to the boardroom. Being there by his side at those meetings, I'd watch people get so heated over issues big and small, sometimes shouting or even crying, but he never let his emotions steer the ship. He'd listen to their problems, their complaints, and their accusations with a super calm demeanor that let everyone know he was in charge. He heard them out, weighed each situation, and spoke only when he was ready. And when he spoke, everyone listened. He presented logical solutions without becoming entangled in reactions.

"You don't get wrapped up in all their fuss," he told me, "because nothing productive comes of it. Sit back, observe, consider within yourself, formulate a decision, and then present it. Don't just jump in, because you're going to say something you don't mean, especially when there's a bunch of money on the line. Just take a breath."

He wasn't a loud guy, or an arrogant one. He never spoke much, even outside the office—unless he had a couple drinks in him, and he'd get funnier the tipsier he was. He came from Missouri and had a southern drawl at times, so he'd say things like "Mizurah" and "Warsh your clothes." Not the most articulate person, and he cussed like a southern boy. But even in the presence of strangers, say at a random table at dinner, he would speak and everyone would turn to listen. He had the ability to gain instant respect from those around him, and I will forever be impressed by that.

It seems like many people these days want to be the first to speak, or at least the loudest, about topics they don't understand. Social media gives everyone a chance to jump in with whatever opinion they might have—no matter how unintelligent or uninformed. We need more people who hold back and consider the situation, people who keep their emotions in check while they seek solutions. In other words: more depth, less volume.

Dad was incredible in that he was able to teach me so much over such a short period of time. I found—and still find—myself in awe of him. We'd walk out of a meeting and I'd immediately begin launching questions at him about everything from ROIs to seating arrangements. There was one particular meeting where the topic was the remodeling of an apartment building, but the Coastal Commission had blocked construction, telling the company they required a new seawall before moving forward.

Building a seawall is no small endeavor, and this one would cost over a million dollars, but they didn't have an extra million dollars in the budget. My dad had a habit of partnering with people who weren't as successful as he was, so everyone looked to him to solve the problem by guaranteeing the loan.

An integral unspoken lesson gleaned from watching my dad work was that being the wealthiest person in the room means you're expected to swoop in and save the day, every time. But what no one acknowledges is that, if things go downhill, you're also the one the lawsuits come for. It doesn't matter whose name is on the paperwork: if you have the most money, you're the target. That means the person with the most money has to be the most cautious, which is why he always withheld his involvement until he was sure the course was safe. My dad practiced that same discernment and caution in all aspects of his life.

***

I was in the middle of my concert promotion business at twenty-three, and it was doing very well, but something lurked in the shadows. I knew something was wrong at home because it was near the holidays and I kept trying to call my dad to say, "Merry Christmas" and "Happy New Year," but I couldn't get ahold of him. *We're both just busy*, I told myself. But two weeks passed and I still hadn't heard from him, so I got on a plane and came back to LA. I drove to the house and finally spoke with him in person.

"I've been delaying this conversation," he told me. "I didn't want to spoil your holidays with this news, but it turns out I have pancreatic cancer, and it doesn't look good."

When his words hit me, along with the knowledge that he would only say them if they were true, the world shifted for me. My dad was sick. Really sick. I could stay in LA, selling out venues for deejays, or I could go back on tour as a band manager, or I could be near my family at a time when they needed me. I made a decision on the spot and called my partner to let her know that the business was hers. I'd help manage the books if she wanted, but I needed to be there for my father. Within twenty-four hours, all ties to my previous life were severed.

Less than a week after I moved home, Dad was hospitalized.

While Dad underwent treatment, I had some big decisions to make. I didn't want to take over the family business, because I'd just spent five years growing my own, but there was no one else who could. If I didn't assume the role, someone else would come in, break up the business, and sell it off. At that time, part of my sisters' incomes came from the company. Should I step in and try to protect my father's legacy, or let it go to pursue my own path?

I chose to protect my family, and that's a decision I'll never regret making. I dove in headfirst, because that's just how I am. When I commit to something, I do it fully.

The existing president of the company had been there for thirty years and was able to mentor me in Dad's place for a time. The clock was ticking for my father, and I had to get to work. Every day, I woke up at 5 a.m., went to the gym for an hour, went to work until 5 p.m., arrived at the hospital to be with my father until 11:30 or midnight, then went home to bed. Next day, same thing all over again. I had no life outside of these responsibilities. Dad told me, "You need to get out of here. This can't be all you do. Go have fun." The thing is, I didn't want another life anymore. I went 100 percent to learn everything I could as quickly as I could. I wanted to make him proud, but I also wanted to prove to myself that I could do it.

The pressure was like nothing else I had experienced. It was multifaceted—my success or failure now meant my whole family's success or failure. I was twenty-three years old—just a kid to most of the people at corporate—and they didn't quite know what to do with me in the beginning. On my first day at the company, they had me put pricing stickers on the menu board in the conference room. I couldn't believe it. They might as well have handed me a coloring book and put me in the corner with a juice box. I realized that if I was going to fill this role, I had to take action of my own accord. My skill set from my concert promotion business was essentially all marketing, so that was my base. I moved myself to the bottom rung of the marketing department at Wienerschnitzel, and that's where I truly started to fit in.

Sitting in the hospital room with Dad one day, about a week before he died, we chatted about a new upcoming corn dog promotion that we were testing before its release. The promotion included some new wording on the corn dog bag that said, "Cash In on a Corn Dog." Our name brand wasn't on the bag; it actually had Foster Farms because they were on the manufacturing side.

Still our recipe, but they produced the corn dogs for us privately. So the head of marketing at the time struck a deal where, rather than Wienerschnitzel paying for packaging, Foster Farms would print the bags for free if they could put their logo on the outside.

Since Dad wasn't able to be present for all the meetings and day-to-day stuff, he relied on me to fill him in on what was happening with the company. We'd talk about things every evening, and I told him about the Foster Farms situation.

"I don't get it," I told him. "Corn dog bags can't be that expensive. Our logo isn't even on the bag and we're advertising Foster Farms instead of our own brand, so how was this a good idea?"

"What?" he said, sitting up in bed. "Are you kidding me? Let me see this bag."

I didn't have one on me, but I brought him a sample bag the next day. He looked at it in disgust and immediately called the head of marketing.

"Ted, John here. Why is our logo not on these bags? These are our bags. The customers are coming to our restaurants. This isn't a Foster Farms outlet."

I knew what Ted was saying on the other end because I'd heard it earlier.

"Well, the bags are free and we're trying to save money in the budget."

"Let me be real clear," said John Galardi. "You change this back to our logo or you don't show up to work tomorrow."

Holy crap, I thought as he hung up the phone. *This man*

is possibly on his literal death bed, and this is the smallest thing compared to his other concerns. But it didn't matter the size of the issue. That company was his baby, and brand integrity was something he didn't budge an inch on. What I learned in that moment was that my father didn't compromise what he cared about, no matter the situation. Saving a little money to sell out his vision simply wasn't a possibility.

Things went downhill pretty quickly for Dad's health. The cancer in his pancreas was killing him and it had to be removed. The doctors presented him with the decision to undergo a Whipple procedure. If you already know what that is, I'm sorry for what you went through. For anyone else who might not know, a Whipple surgery is where the doctors cut open the patient and essentially take all their organs out and set them aside, then remove all the cancer from the pancreas, and finally put all the organs back in and stitch the patient up. It's the equivalent of very carefully ripping the human body apart. At the time, the survival rate for the surgery itself was under 25 percent due to its invasiveness. Even if he made it through that, the chance of surviving pancreatic cancer was 5 percent.

As previously demonstrated by me, the Galardis have never been too impressed by bad odds, so Dad chose to have the procedure.

He survived the surgery and we thought he was out of the woods. Of course we did, because this man was a legend. Naturally, *the* John Galardi would be in that 5 percent of survivors. The world just kept throwing survival rates at us, and we just kept batting them over the fence. He'd be back in the office within a month, making deals and tending his corporate baby.

But he still had to undergo chemo. The Whipple surgery succeeded at cutting and scraping all the cancer out of him, but the microscopic cancer cells could only be removed with chemotherapy, which takes significant strength to endure.

Dad never recovered from his surgery enough to get the chemo. He was on life support for two days and almost rallied, but the shock to his system was simply too much for him. He was still coherent, but there was nothing more the doctors could do for him. The cancer cells ran rampant through his body and attacked everywhere, and that's what killed him in the end.

He died on April 13, 2013.

We went around the room and each of us leaned in to whisper in his ear. I told him I loved him. We were told when we left that we'd never see him again, but I kept up hope that we had more time. Not knowing what else to do, we went to lunch. Then I got a text saying that he was gone. We rushed back to the room, but it was too late.

All these years later and I still can't talk about it.

The morning after he passed, I was walking around at home trying to find a sense of normalcy in my world. My heart hurt, but I kept hearing my dad's voice saying, "You've got to get your shit together. You've got to work. You can't lay around." I thought about my father, and what he had built, and where it stood now. I thought about the people whose lives he'd changed. I thought about all of those restaurants around the country and imagined

them empty and lifeless.

I showered, I got dressed, and I went to work. I walked into the office to find grieving employees mourning the loss of a beloved man.

In some ways, I thought, *they knew him better than I did.*

I received a lot of handshakes, hugs, and shared tears, but I also saw a lot of fear in their eyes. These people had depended on my father, and I was there to show them that they could depend on me, too. No one had to worry that the company would be sold off and everyone fired.

No matter what was happening in my personal life, I was there for them.

John Galardi (left), in his 30s, and JR Galardi (right), age 25, in front of the Wienerschnitzel store.

Taking the Helm

13

In the grand scheme of Wienerschnitzel, I'm a blip on the radar. It's a historic brand. We just celebrated our 60th anniversary and things are going very well, but they were going pretty well before I showed up, too. I've made some improvements and contributions, but it hasn't been an easy road—which might surprise some people. My own business endeavor was a success, and I didn't want to set it aside for anyone or anything. How could I put my dream on hold to live someone else's? I had my own empire to build, and it was well on its way.

Then cancer killed my dad.

I am where I am because of nepotism. I recognize that. If I had applied to Galardi Group as an outsider, I might be holding a higher position in marketing at this point, but that's probably as far as I'd have made it. That's not an admission that I'm unequipped to be in charge, merely a recognition of the truth about my situation. The knowledge that I was handed something that most others couldn't attain only drives me harder to prove that I won't ruin this chance. I'm not going to kick back and let things drift past while others run the show.

When Dad passed away, the corporate structure stayed exactly the same, except my mom became the new CEO. That's what my dad wanted, which, unsurprisingly, shocked a lot of people because who leaves stuff to their ex-wife? Yet, he had insisted that it should go to my mom. Mom had been there through some of the company's toughest trials and tribulations; she had seen and heard everything John Galardi had heard for decades and had been his confidant. John, having always been keenly aware that he would need to create a succession plan and leave the reins of Wienerschnitzel in capable hands, understood that she would do what was best, not only for the company, but for his children. Whether that meant selling the business or holding onto it, she would know what to do. He hoped that I would take the helm, but it would be up to my mom to decide if, and when, I was ready.

My mom is the sweetest lady ever; she's a saint. An angel. But if she thinks you're not doing a good job, she'll cut you off, feelings be damned. That's how she managed raising her family and how she approached running the company. Her style of management is what most people would recognize as micromanaging, because she wasn't sure where she should put her trust and expected everyone to prove themselves all over again. Her methods required her to question everything and become deeply entrenched in the minutiae of how everyone did their jobs, and that rubbed a lot of people the wrong way—including me.

I understand that it was a difficult time for her. Even though they hadn't been together for some time, she had just lost a very important person in her life, and I'm sure the grieving process impacted her deeply. On top of that, she had suddenly been thrust into a demanding, high-pressure position where everyone was looking to her for answers and leadership. It had to have been tough on her. She rose to the challenge, but she got so wrapped up in taking the reins that it overrode her better judgment. There was no trust for her employees because, in her eyes, they hadn't earned it yet, even though they had already proven their loyalty and value to the company for years. It was so vastly different from what everyone was used to, and since there was no gradual lead up to it, she alienated a lot of people. Seeing it happen just ate away at my core.

Within a month, Mom had taken all the furniture out of Dad's office and redone it to match her style, which, to those of us on the outside looking in, only served to symbolize her undoing of my dad's progress. I don't blame her for wanting a fresh start, but the way she went about it felt abrasive and jolting because I wasn't ready to move on from having my dad in charge. She got so carried away with being in charge that she overlooked something critical: Dad didn't expect her to run the company, just hold onto it.

We clashed, she and I. She wanted to be perceived as a leader while moving the company forward with new ideas and enthusiasm, but the staff was still in mourning and not ready or open to her style of change. I could see it was causing conflicts from so many different perspectives, not just my own. I listened to the complaints of my coworkers and came to her with advice to redirect, but she wasn't willing to listen. She refused to see our team for what it was: the true reason for our success. She felt that she owed it to Dad to make the company even more successful, but in the meantime, she forgot that she still had a grieving son with no one else to turn to. She had lost her husband, but I had lost my father; together, we had a responsibility to handle his legacy the right way, and this wasn't it.

All the moving parts of this overall conflict culminated into a confrontation between us. She called in a bunch of consultants and planned to replace one of the people who had really helped make the company what it was, someone who had been with us for decades, with her lead consultant. But this consultant, from everything I could see, had no idea what he was doing. He couldn't even calculate speed of service, which is one of the most fundamental aspects of the job. He was a bad fit.

I went into her office, closed the door behind me, and told her, in no uncertain terms, that I did not support her decision. I felt so strongly about it that, if she followed through with this plan, I was leaving. I couldn't sit there a moment longer watching her Ready-Fire-Aim (pull the trigger before thinking things through) approach to running the company. It wasn't what Dad wanted, or what I wanted, and I had other prospects to pursue if push came to shove. I'd slept on a floor and I'd do it again if I had to, but all I really wanted was for her to take a step back and try a different approach.

Not all parents can handle when their adult child takes a tone with them the way I did. I realize that she could have taken my words two different ways: either my threatening to leave showed that I'm too irresponsible to be trusted, or the fact that I took a stand proved that I was ready for leadership. How must it have looked to her, to see the little boy she used to pay with quarters to go to time out suddenly speaking to her as a man and telling her how to behave? Whatever went on inside her mind, she finally agreed to ease up. We had many, many more conversations about the path I wanted to take, and over time, she grew to trust not only me, but the team we built together. And Dad's furniture? Mom actually saved it and gave it to me as a gift. Dad's desk is the same one I use today.

One statistic I came across at that time was that the median age of our customer demographic was forty-eight years old. All things considered, that's pretty old for a median customer base. Anyone I talked to said the same thing: "Oh, I used to go to Wienerschnitzel after little league when I was a kid. I didn't know you were still in business. You guys are still around?" As a startup with a fifty-year platform, we weren't moving forward into the next generation. If we didn't adapt soon, we'd be a distant memory in the food industry.

I brought the matter up to our president, my mom, and

everyone on the board. I told them we needed to make a big shift in our marketing, because our customers were loyal and nostalgic about Wienerschnitzel, but they were also aging.

"We're not marketing to millennials," I said. "I'm a millennial, which should be our target demographic, and I have some ideas that I think could help bridge this gap. Let me market to myself."

I turned to the VP of marketing, who'd been with the company for thirty years at the time, and said, "I can't find the Wienerschnitzel Instagram or any of our social media presence."

His response: "The what now?"

Clearly, we had a problem: we weren't evolving.

During this time, I was still in lower-level marketing doing PowerPoint presentations, drafting memos, and traveling around to various franchises to present marketing plans. Anyone could have done the job, but I wanted to do more. I went through an eight-week training program where I became a franchisee of one of our restaurants to learn the operational side of the company. It was a good experience, and I soaked up all the information I could. When I came back from those two months in the field, I had a fresh set of ideas on how we could improve our sales.

After some discussion on the matter, they agreed to put me back in the marketing department, and they wanted my input on how to navigate the changes I proposed. I shuffled a lot of people around, moving some up to operational roles, pulling some from the field, and replacing those who needed to go. Unfortunately, the VP of marketing had to be replaced. It wasn't an easy thing to recommend, because many of these people had been with the company for decades, but at the same time, we had to look to our future growth. Decisions had to be made. They were still budgeting heavily for print and radio advertising, which are rather antiquated relics from yesteryear in the world of marketing; that didn't mean we had to eliminate them, only expand them. Just because something worked in the past doesn't mean it will continue to do so, and the only way to keep progressing is to identify what stagnates you and remove it. Just as Dad had done before, I had to keep us moving for the good of the company.

We needed fresh, new blood. I had interned for a man named Doug Koegeboehn at an ad agency when I was a teenager, and since I was really impressed by him, I went over and recruited him. Doug is now our CMO. We started a social media campaign, got an Instagram presence, and launched the Facebook page. With a little digging, we discovered a customer email database of half a million addresses, so we sent out promotions and coupons in droves.

Within a year, our median age dropped to forty-five. That doesn't seem like a big swing for the average person, but you have to keep in mind we pull in about three million transactions per month. A three-year shift in customer age is pretty huge when you take all those sales into account. What that meant was that our efforts were paying out: younger customers were coming in the door every day. We were able to see quantifiable evidence that our changes were making a difference.

One of the pitfalls of being the boss' kid is that people in the company aren't inclined to believe that telling you the truth is in their best interests. Not all of my ideas were solid gold, so I watched for the people who could look past who I was on paper, skip the politeness of responding to "the boss' son," and give me a no-bullshit reaction. Dennis Tase (president), Ken Wagstaff (CFO), Doug Koegeboehn (CMO), Bob Matthews (VP of Legal and Development), and Rusty Bills (VP of Operations) were five experts who'd give it to me straight every time. If I threw out a dumb idea, they'd call it what it was and tell me to go back to the drawing board. The six of us developed an amazing rapport. Doug especially has a knack for quickly telling me why certain things will or won't work, but he's so tactful about how he does it. He worked at an advertising agency for many years as a client rep, so he knows how to maneuver without disagreeing outright, but his tact is always upheld by open honesty, which is an asset I value greatly. Ken, on the other hand, will say things like, "You're an idiot. Wingsuit flying in Europe isn't a tax write-off." If only it were, Ken.

Galardi Group was basically like an old regime. What happens in the US when a new president gets elected? Anyone attached to the former president is gone, replaced by the new order. Eventually, roughly 50 percent of the executive administration was replaced, filtered out either through retirement or firing, to make way for a team of like-minded individuals who could match stride with the fresh outlook.

The transition from marketing to president of the company was a six-year period, and it was during this time that I truly found a passion for our brand. As I proved myself time and again, I was promoted to higher positions. I gave everything I had to every job I held, absorbing as much as I could learn each day, and I knew my perseverance was paying off. According to the plan established by the company, I went from marketing manager to our Visionary department (more on that later), then director of Hamburger Stand, then director of operations for Galardi Group, then VP of operations, then director of administration, vice president, and finally president after Dennis retired.

"It is often said, though, that if you achieve your goals, you haven't set them high enough." This nugget of wisdom from the first half of the book holds a relevant truth in my life and how I develop my personal goals, both short term and long term. Long-term goals are essential, but they're built on the fundamental concept of progress. My long-term goal is to eventually take over my mother's role as CEO, but that decision is fully in her hands. For the time being, I'm quite pleased with my progress, and the experience of seeing my dedication pay off has been empowering. Wienerschnitzel runs in my blood, and those six years were only a small sample of the business education I'd gotten from my father's subtle coaching my entire life. One could say I was made for this job, despite the long road it took to get there. I've had plenty of setbacks, but each of them was just another chance to prove myself.

One particular chance—a "boss moment," if you will—occurred while we were in New York City with the majority of our management team. I was still in marketing at the time, but

I'd been asked to attend and learn the ropes of other aspects of the business. We were all sitting down together to meet with the bank to discuss some upcoming plans and essentially hash out how various people performed in their roles.

The team lead turned to me and said, "Say you're in charge today. You're the one calling the shots, and whatever you say goes, hypothetically. What would you do?"

My immediate response was, "I would fire this person, this person, and this person. I would promote this person and this person and put them in these specific roles that play to their strengths, and I'd do it today."

I must have said the right things, because over the course of the next year, all the things I recommended happened, and those individuals I said should be promoted have absolutely killed it and gotten promoted even higher. But those executives could have easily ignored everything I had to say. They could have said, "That's nice, kid, but the grownups are talking now." I wasn't recommending small things; some of the people I said I'd fire had been with the company for ten or more years. One in particular had been there for thirty years. Clearly they held some value to the team I'd addressed, right? They'd been around for decades and were probably close friends with the men and women on the management team gathered around me. As I look back on it now, what I did was pretty risky, but it paid off.

As those old regime employees parted ways, that's when it really sank in that my words carried weight and my opinions mattered. Mom, as the CEO, had the deciding vote on anything at that level, but she wouldn't have followed my advice without the full confidence of the executive team. For them to have confidence in my proposed plan was a phenomenal compliment, but it also meant that my actions could affect people's lives.

And that was terrifying.

Machiavellianism doesn't always prevail. You have to create a space where your team feels comfortable brainstorming ideas without judgment. These days, I don't just make decisions and tell people to deal with it. I understand that my decisions matter—they affect people other than myself and those in my immediate circle. I'm not a dictator tossing out commands. No one on my team is afraid to share their opinions or provide input. We work together and trust one another to do the best job we know how. Building that team has taken considerable effort, but I've followed my instincts at every turn. Some people just feel right; others don't. The ability to identify who's right for a certain position and who's not is what can easily make or break a company. Is someone underperforming? Is there another person you know who might be a better fit? Just because I'm in charge doesn't mean I should be able to do your job better than you. I hired you because you're great at what you do. I should be learning from you. It's basically a two-way mentoring relationship with both of us reaching for our full potential. So I surround myself with people who can move the company where it needs to go.

Operating a successful business is not all smiles and handshakes, however. Like any business, there are times when things go wrong and I have to step in and calm the waters. Most of the time, it's just dealing with frustrated franchisees who just need to vent. The difference between us and, say, Starbucks or Chick-fil-A, is that we're 100 percent franchised. The franchisees, who have a personal investment in their restaurants, pay us (Galardi Group) to fix their problems, and problems will inevitably arise no matter what.

To reiterate John Galardi's purpose, the franchisees are the heart of the Wienerschnitzel family.

At the end of the day, it's our job as executives to listen to our franchisees, but if they're disrespectful or otherwise hostile, I'll come back at them hard. Raised voices are nothing; that shows they care about their situation and are in need of assistance. They're not really yelling at me anyway; they're yelling at their issues. I've been with the company long enough that nothing in the franchise realm shakes me up anymore. I've seen it all before, and they just want to feel heard when it's all said and done.

Sometimes, as in any realm with a pecking order, the boss has to be the boss, and that usually means firing someone. That's a very real aspect of my responsibilities, and I must be the person to do it, but I hate it so much. There's a protocol to follow, which is helpful for me, but that doesn't make it any easier. To sit across from a person and say, "You're done working with us," is something I'll never get accustomed to no matter how many times it happens. Before calling them in, I try to go through the motions of the conversation internally to set in my mind how I want the interaction to go. I ask myself, "What's the best decision for the company?" and if that employee isn't part of that best decision, they have to go. You have to learn how to separate your emotional reactions from the logic behind firing them, and it can be extremely difficult in some cases.

One instance in particular stands out to me. There was a woman who had been with the company for thirty years, but I felt her time with us had come to an end. It wasn't a decision I came to lightly, and I'm not just saying that. She'd worked with Galardi Group longer than I'd been alive. Her job was her livelihood, and I had to take it away. It makes me sound like a monster, but there's another side to the equation.

As time went on, I began to realize that what work she did get done was done incorrectly, so I specifically stopped giving her any work to do. I let that go on for a while because I felt sorry for her, but it reached a point that I couldn't ignore it any longer. I looked through her file and saw that she'd been moved from department to department over the years. We couldn't continue paying her to do nothing, no matter how sweet she might be.

We set up a meeting with the director of HR and I told her right away, "We're having this conversation because you're not performing at your job to the best of your ability. We've given you X amount of warnings and have decided to remove the position. I want you to know I've really enjoyed our time together, but this is the right decision. Thank you for being a part of our family for so long, and I wish you all the very best."

For her and many others, we typically show our love by providing a great severance package, so I let her know that

would be coming her way. She cried a little and then I ended the meeting, but afterward she sent me a really nice email saying she appreciated everything we did for her. I've had other people throw tantrums in front of me, so it meant a lot that she could part ways with such grace.

Once the moment's over, though, the finality of the choice settles in and brings with it all the doubt and guilt over cutting ties with someone you've known for years. Was it premature? Did we do everything we could to avoid termination? Was there another option on the table that we didn't consider? Was I wrong? This is the part I dread the most, because I know how fallible I am as a person. I'm not perfect; I make mistakes like anyone else, but was this one of them? The only way to know for sure is through time, then learn from the ordeal for the next one, because it's coming.

Experience brings wisdom, and I needed that wisdom to steer the ship.

JR Galardi serving hot dogs

Ebb and Flow

14

The pandemic was the hardest challenge I had ever faced at Wienerschnitzel, but there were a lot of factors at play in our success.

Unemployment rose drastically during COVID. Between the stimulus checks and other forms of assistance, people could make more money sitting at home than they could in the workforce. And I get it, because that was a pandemic and no one was really sure what would happen, but the problem is that it demotivated many who might otherwise have found success; it allowed people to stop relying on their jobs for income. Everyone started looking for new ways to make money without coming in to work. So the restaurants had far fewer employees present, and yet our sales continued to skyrocket. That meant customers wanted more food—due to grocery stores struggling to keep stocked, or stress eating, or any number of other reasons—but we just didn't have enough workers on site to meet the demand.

We saw a huge dip in crew members. They called in sick for weeks on end because of the bill the government passed that allowed workers to take time off without losing sick days or vacation days. The bill stated that employees didn't have to prove they had COVID, only that they suspected they might, and they could take two weeks off and still collect full pay. Once that window passed, the employees began showing back up to work again, miraculously COVID-free. Then, the bill was reinstated, and the numbers dropped yet again.

The day they released the first stimulus checks, we had twenty truck drivers quit on the spot. Our distribution center almost came to a halt. Sales were still climbing, but the restaurants couldn't get the deliveries they needed on time. They were burning through food at record speed but weren't able to replace their supplies. Even if a truck did arrive, many locations didn't have staff on hand to unload it. Other locations had people ready to unload, but no trucks.

Our corporate phones blew up. Everyone was freaking out, looking for answers and solutions to recoup their losses and get back on track. I oversaw a conference call between some of our LA franchisees and two of the account service reps at the distribution center where the LA franchisees were yelling at the account reps, who have no control over what's going on, all the while they're looking to Galardi Group as the contract holders to keep the distribution company accountable and make sure the food is delivered on time to our franchisees. With everything going on during a pandemic, we weren't able to control whether employees showed up to the distribution center, just like we can't control whether employees show up to Wienerschnitzel restaurants.

So I let them all vent for a while.

As much as I would have liked to step in on the side of our franchisees, I had to take a neutral-but-stern approach of reprimanding and encouraging both sides at once. Relationships have to be maintained, and siding with one or the other would have unbalanced the situation further, which was something none of us could afford at the time. Once the anger passed and they stopped assigning undeserved blame, we were able to re-engage and make a plan of action.

Incidentally, John Galardi, the visionary, had prepped us for a huge win during 2020. Wienerschnitzel's drive-thru model, which my dad introduced sixty years ago, was a major contributing factor to our success during COVID. Unintentionally, Dad had created a perfect fast-food system for pandemic lockdowns. So many other businesses had to close down, and many of them never recovered enough to reopen. In a normal year, on average, 60 percent of our business goes through the drive thru. Most of our restaurants were using the drive-thru for the majority of their sales, so all we really had to do during the lockdown was close our dining room, which allowed us to refocus the other 40 percent into the avenue we already knew very well. With a little ingenuity, and admittedly a little luck, we were able to stay open at a time that people needed us.

To give some understanding of what I mean when I say our sales skyrocketed, let me share some numbers. When I came into the business full-time, our sales at the time were about $200 million per year. That's not profit, just total sales. In 2020, we were about $330 million. This year, in 2021, we're on track for probably $360 million. That's almost double where we were just a few years prior, but it's nothing I can take sole credit for. I've done my part and made a difference, sure, but my team is responsible for such overwhelming success. They fought hard during the pandemic, and it paid out big time.

To clarify, all of these sales are same-store sales. In other words, we aren't making more money because we've opened more Wienerschnitzels, but because we're driving more traffic to our existing stores. Long wait times mean frustrated customers who'll go elsewhere, so we've increased operational efficiency and prioritized certain things to get more throughput in each restaurant. We've put a huge emphasis on improving the customer experience at the store level, which includes visual appeal. All our stores look good inside and out. The dining rooms are updated so they don't look thirty years old anymore. The equipment we use is modern. The goal there was to re-energize the brand, which I can say in full confidence we have done.

Another key aspect of customer experience we have improved is our face-to-face service. Things like friendliness in our staff, greeting and warmth, order accuracy, turnaround times, etc. We've developed a culture where everyone who enters one of our restaurants should have the best minute of their day while interacting with one of our staff. Anyone who might be having a dreary day should be able to pull up to a Wienerschnitzel, or walk inside, and have one of the employees greet them with a smile and a hello within three seconds; it should be a nice break from that dreary day, every time. Our whole mission statement now is serving food to serve others, and the more money we can make, the more money we can use to help people. It's why we show up to work every day.

And those aren't empty words to gain false morale. We've implemented a program where, if employees volunteer their time on weekends, they can submit those volunteer hours to earn vacation time with the company. So if you're giving your personal time to help others at a local homeless shelter or food bank, that's equating to time off from work. If employees want to donate to a charity, we will match their donation up to a certain amount. We've also incorporated a scholarship fund for anyone related to a Wienerschnitzel employee. It doesn't matter if it's their second cousin; that person can apply for the scholarship. All of these things carry our mission to promote a caring family atmosphere where the reason to show up to work is more than just laboring toward a paycheck. It's having a great impact on our teams, and I think that feeling of togetherness translates directly to the customer's perception of our brand.

We've always shown resilience over the years, making it through lockdowns, pandemics, and recessions alike. Unlike something like COVID, a financial crash goes straight for people's wallets. Everyone lives leaner during a recession. Fine dining went to casual dining, and casual dining went to fast food, and fast food went to eating at home more often. We're also commodities-based, which means we're somewhat at the mercy of prices on items like gasoline or corn. If one of our commodities has a price spike or drop, we have to adapt to the climate. We tighten our belts like all the rest, and we make it through.

Political factors are huge these days, and we make it a point to stay clear of that minefield. Chick-fil-A took their stance on being anti-gay and opted to stay closed on Sundays, and they're still feeling the brunt of cancel culture from that. We keep out of politics because it has nothing to do with our food. We just stay in our lane and keep doing what we love doing.

I've mentioned adapting a few times, which is critical for any successful business, and one of the places we've really focused on adapting is the Wienerschnitzel menu. A diverse menu is one that will last, because it's constantly shifting to match the needs of our customers. The first Wienerschnitzel menu was fairly limited in comparison to what we use today; for example, it didn't offer burgers and had chips instead of fries. We keep our core items and play around with the fringe items.

The Wienerschnitzel R&D department is always hard at work. It's headed by one woman who knows food very well, and she uses her experience as a chef and food scientist to constantly create new products. She's done the same for many other companies and had a consulting firm to help make some decisions, but now she works alongside my purchasing department (who track costs for ingredients) and one of my directors of operations (who is there to make sure everything is operationally feasible at the restaurant level). Together, they conceptualize fresh ideas with unique flavor profiles, then present them to our marketing team (which includes me) to figure out how to best move the new product, how long everything takes to cook, how many stations are required, how much workers need to move to compile everything, and so on. We have to consider the throughput of the restaurant, and if the recipe requires staff to bump into one another between the grill and the cheese station, that recipe has to change. I personally taste and critique everything on our menu, sometimes calling for improvements or changes as needed. Most of the time, though, they knock it out of the park.

Sometimes the process goes the other direction, and it's important that it can work both ways. Our marketing team will present an idea to R&D that we think will do well or a flavor that might be trending, so they set to work building the menu to match our vision. One recent promotion revolved around featuring hot dogs from around the world. R&D did some research on different locales and started compiling prototypes for us to taste test. We all loved the bratwurst from Germany with mustard, choice of sauerkraut or grilled onions, and a soft pretzel bun, so we added that in time for Oktoberfest.

R&D went out on a limb and put together a Polish hot dog topped up with cheese, bacon, jalapeños, grilled onions, and a horseradish aioli. It was so good that I just kept eating the samples. We weren't sure what to call it at first, but we looked into

Australian flavors and found that they use jalapeños, so it just went under "Australia" until we settled on Aussie Dog. Some were more straightforward, like the Texas, Kansas City, and Carolina BBQ Dogs with—you guessed it—barbecue sauce; but others, like the Sonoran Dog from Mexico, with bacon, pinto beans, tomatoes, mustard, mayo, and jalapeños, had a uniqueness all their own. One of our top sellers, the Chicago Dog, comes loaded with tomatoes, fresh onions, pickle spears, relish, sport peppers, mustard, and sprinkled with celery salt to finish. The thing is a work of art.

For the record, my personal order is two corn dogs, two chili dogs. When I worked at the Wienerschnitzel franchise, I always got two corn dogs and two chili dogs every day for lunch for the entire summer. They're just too good. Maybe I should tell R&D we need to run a JR Special . . .

Even just reading about these products makes people's mouths water, so you can imagine the effect inside the restaurant. Back in the day, my dad would just grill onions all day because something about the smell of cooked onions makes people hungry. Customers would smell the onions and come in to satisfy their cravings. If you've ever been to a mall, you've probably smelled Cinnabon right off the bat and, chances are, you went and bought one. They used to take the bakery smell and pump it around the building to trigger people's senses. Same concept with the onions, only these days, our HVAC systems are too advanced for tactics like that; they just filter out all the good smells and the onions never make it outside the building.

Time, economic change, social media marketing—so many of the elements that wear a company down or drown it in a sea of competitors as it ages—have only revealed that most of the things that Dad innovated are still in use, like the red-and-yellow advertising. Dad always said that those two colors make people hungry, and years later, studies have confirmed exactly that over and over. Everything I do today is an expansion of his original ideas in one way or another, but I've also been able to put my own spin on things.

***

Dad had always known, in his time, what appealed to his target demographic. He made Wienerschnitzel a hip place long before internet influencers were a thing. He created fleets of OG influencers by seeking out the cool kids and getting them to work at a Wienerschnitzel, getting them to spread the word about how cool and great it was, and watching the natural marketing spread like wildfire amongst that generation. I strive to do the exact same thing—just modernized to fit the times.

In all my experience prior to Dad's passing, I learned so much about marketing to millennials from energy drink companies. Who speaks to that generation better than Monster? Nobody does. Monster's whole premise on energy drinks started out with sampling. Let people try your stuff and then hope they go buy more of it.

A friend of mine had previously worked at Monster, and I

offered him a job to help us get into sports marketing, which he accepted right away. He and I worked together with Dennis to come up with a name for the department, but we just couldn't find the right fit. One day, Dennis and I were walking down the street in Manhattan and this guy walked past us wearing a baseball cap that said "Visionary" on it. Dennis and I looked at each other and both said, "Visionary department," and that was that. We had our name.

While looking into more of that millennial campaigning, I did some research and found out that 33 percent of Supercross and Motocross fans eat fast food more than three times per week. So I sponsored a Supercross team, which allowed us to enter all their events. The Visionary department started partnering with Supercross, and everything went ballistic from there. We created an activation team that would go to events—everything from surfing to skating—and hand out free hot dogs to everybody who wanted one. Their job was to just cook hot dogs and give them away as fast as they could. We commissioned some trucker hats to hand out as well, which all said "I ♡ Wieners" with a little Wienerschnitzel logo in the heart, and it was all wildly successful. From then on, whenever extreme sports got attention, so did Wienerschnitzel.

The old regime could never have anticipated this move, nor the payout that came with it, which is why change is so crucial to a thriving business. They couldn't even see the changes they needed to make, let alone make them. The old ways should never survive long enough to be called "the old ways." It's my life's goal to never become stagnant, and that's why I always look to the future—but that future comes with questions.

Who cares about hot dogs? At the end of the day, as tasty as they may be, hot dogs don't matter. What matters is why you get out of bed in the morning. Why do you go to work? Why do you do what you do? Inevitably, the questions roll past yourself, because you're just a person and your time is finite. The question you have to ask yourself is: "Who are you helping?"

You can help a lot of people by giving up your own time, but as I said, your time is finite. What can truly make a lasting impact on helping others is money. I'm not talking about handouts or change jars by the cash register. I could stand on the street corner throwing dollar bills all day and not make a difference in a single life. I could give a thousand dollars to everyone I passed until I ran out, but even that won't alleviate suffering. Money can only accomplish great things if it's focused on those who stand in need.

Ever since my mom and I took the reins of Galardi Group, we've gotten more involved in the philanthropic side of the company. We're just like any other corporate structure, except we have an official philanthropy department that's been around since 2015. We agreed long ago that the more success we have at selling hot dogs, the more money we can direct to help others. For example, we partner with Rock Solid Foundation, which builds playgrounds for kids with pediatric cancer—kids who can't leave their homes and have forgotten what play is because their entire lives are just endless doctor appointments. They've lost what it means to be a child. So we go to their houses and build them a place to remember.

We've done a lot with homeless outreach, and we're getting heavily involved in Operation Underground Railroad, which is an anti-child-trafficking organization. My mom is also very passionate about literacy for children, and she helps coordinate our philanthropy department in that direction.

Hot dogs can make the world a better place with the right people making the right decisions.

***

Another friend of mine, Mike Smith, started a program called Skate for Change, where he would skateboard around Lincoln, Nebraska, and give socks to the homeless. One thing many people don't realize is that being homeless puts you at significant risk of boot rot, or trench foot. Prolonged exposure to moisture in cold, damp, often unsanitary conditions creates restricted blood flow to the feet and starts the breakdown of tissues in as little as ten hours. Soldiers had to deal with it mostly back in WWI, but it's still affecting people all around us. A homeless person who is sitting down likely isn't doing so because they're lazy, or tired, or hungover, as many people seem to think. Rather, it's probably because their feet hurt so badly.

Mike found all this out because he talked to the homeless like they were people rather than treating them like a disease or mistake. Mike played basketball for the University of Nebraska, and he'd go into the locker room after games to find boxes and boxes of socks from various sporting goods sponsors, all just sitting there in case one of the athletes felt like wearing them. So Mike took all the socks and started handing them out to the homeless, which is where they probably should have gone in the first place. What he started in Nebraska, Skate for Change, now has around eighty chapters all over the world, all providing people with a basic necessity that so many others take for granted.

We saw eye to eye, Mike and I, and we became friends by working together with the Children's Hospital during Christmas, as well as many other charities over the years. With his notoriety, he got asked to speak at schools all over the country about his non-profit program, and hearing his story just inspired me to do more. I told Mike one day, "I have access to a whole lot of food vendors and delivery services. I can get food shipped basically anywhere. What should we do?"

We brainstormed for a while and came up with the idea for Hot Dogs for Homeless. We got our hands on a bus, slapped a Wienerschnitzel logo on it, and, for a month straight, drove it around the country to raise money for Mike's non-profit. We'd arrive at the next school on his schedule, Mike would give his motivational speech, and then any kids who'd volunteered to help would load onto the bus (with parental and administrative permission) to go with us to the impoverished areas of their community. The school would host a fundraiser to fill up bags of supplies, which we'd help the kids deliver to those in need. Mike and I would break out coolers packed with hot dogs and condiments and just cook for everyone who wanted to eat, and of course we'd hand out tons of socks. The looks on those kids' faces were priceless, because each one of them thought the exact same thing: "This is it? This is all I have to do to help people?" I'd tell them all, "It's that easy. Something so small in your day can change a person's day, week, maybe even their year."

Media outlets started hearing about us, so we had morning news interviews at each city, or call-in radio shows where they wanted to hear about what we were doing. Everything snowballed, but it was exhausting. We woke up most days at 3 a.m., drove hard to the next place on the list, did some interviews, went to the school, and talked to the kids. Then it was time to cook hot dogs, hand out the supplies, take donations, clean up, and move on to the next place. Whoever wasn't driving could snatch a couple hours of sleep, but that was about it, day after day. I don't share that as a complaint or anything, because the experience was always amazing, but to demonstrate the level of our commitment.

We held Hot Dogs for Homeless two years in a row for the entire month of April; a full thirty days of service. We hit twenty cities at a time, with Mike and I taking turns driving the bus, and eventually started picking up some of our other friends to help out.

The bus gathered a lot of attention to our cause, and word got out about what we were doing. Celebrities started tweeting about the charity, and even Kelly Osborne made Instagram videos in her smooth British accent, saying, "You've got to go donate to Hot Dogs for Homeless. Get to their website and donate now!" That was a great endorsement because she's also been heavily involved in charity work. Thanks, Kelly!

All this happened under the Visionary department, and it built momentum not only for Mike's charity, but for Wienerschnitzel as well. I'd been putting my work responsibilities on hold to do Hot Dogs for Homeless for two Aprils straight, but I couldn't personally keep doing that without taking my eyes off my company. However, all the groundwork had been laid by Mike and me, so I decided to make things official by hiring my oldest sister, Karen, to run the philanthropy department. She'd never been attached to the company before, so this was a perfect way for her to be involved while helping others.

I think anytime people can associate a business with charity, they'll have a much higher opinion of that business and prefer it over others that don't donate their time and money to helping people. With every town we hit on the bus, our sales spiked in that area. Not to say that was the motivation for helping, because it wasn't, but the increase in sales was definitely a welcome side effect.

Galardi Group functions as an umbrella or parent company to our various subsidiaries. Under that umbrella are Wienerschnitzel, Hamburger Stand, and Tastee-Freez. There is some crossover between the three restaurants—like Tastee-Freez is offered in almost every Wienerschnitzel, and Hamburger Stand has both a Wienerschnitzel menu and Tastee-Freez soft serve—but they are considered separate entities when it comes to business interactions.

These days, Wienerschnitzel is in thirteen states, like Texas,

California, Arizona, Utah, etc. There's so much room to grow, but we focus more on strengthening what we have before branching out to new places. Dennis Tase, who was president of the company for thirty years, retired a while ago, and I took his place. So now I'm both COO and president of Galardi Group. Beneath me is the executive team, which is made up of the CFO, VP of Development and Legal, VP of Operations, and the CMO in charge of marketing.

They all make my job so easy and work so hard to keep all the balls up in the air. Their passion is what keeps the wheels turning for the brand, and I couldn't do it without each of them. I genuinely care about my team as individuals and make it a point to remind them of that often. I think they'd express the same thing if you asked them. We call it the Wiener Fam, because we treat each other like family. We take care of each other. And I think that feeling of being cared for, of being part of a large family, pays out to keep us all motivated to improve every day.

Nobody really has an answer for where we're all headed moving forward, beyond COVID. The pandemic changed so much about how we think as a society, and for me, personally, I don't see a world where I'm in my office 9–5, five days a week. Yes, there are certain times when it's beneficial to be in the office, but the office isn't going anywhere.

I don't want that kind of life anymore, and I don't want that life for my employees; it's just not necessary. It's an old stigma from a (recently) bygone era. If I want to truly show how much I care for the wellbeing of our employees and franchisees, then I have to take action to demonstrate it. We used to think that's just how work had to be, but COVID, as terrible as it was for so many people, forced us to learn we could adapt to new circumstances. If there's a better way to do something, let's do it and not just cling to the old ways because that's how it was always done.

Interview with Fox News in Albuquerque, New Mexico, about Wienerschnitzel's Hot Dogs for Homeless bus.

Kids lining up in front of the Wienerschnitzel bus at Barlett City School in Tennessee. #hotdogs4homeless

Who is JR Galardi?

15

Who am I without my dad? Who is JR Galardi?

I've been asking myself that for a long time. I'm just a guy trying to figure it out. I think that's all any of us are doing.

My childhood was abnormal compared to most people. I mean, it was normal in that my parents were loving figures who cared for my needs, and I went to school and played sports, but abnormal in the way I was raised and the opportunities I was given. I recognize that. The majority of my impressionable growing-up years took place in Aspen, Colorado, which is a ski resort town that most people only visit during winter vacation. The median household income there is something like $115K, and the average cost of a house there is around ten or fifteen million dollars. They have Gucci and Prada stores, and it's not uncommon to bump into celebrities on the street. According to known expert

Lloyd Christmas, Aspen is "a place where the beer flows like wine, where beautiful women instinctively flock like the salmon of Capistrano" (*Dumb & Dumber,* 1994). That's a pretty far cry from learning to survive on the streets of Jaipur.

Thanks to my parents, I grew up with the financial capability to support the things I wanted to do, like snowboarding. I got out of school three days a week to go snowboarding, which most teenagers just can't do. That built my skill in the sport, which increased my interest in it, which allowed me to excel in it. Before long, I was snowboarding competitively.

Dad didn't just operate outside the box with how he raised me, his philosophies crossed over into his business just as well. He implemented a rule many years ago that the corporate office closes early every Friday, which lets everyone get a jump on the weekend and beat rush hour traffic. For the 9–5 crowd, that was an amazing morale booster and unusual in business. I used to rush to the ocean every Friday afternoon so I could start relaxing immediately and not waste a second of that precious weekend time. After COVID hit, everything shut down and stayed closed, including the Galardi Group office, as we all adjusted to the new reality.

I'll be the first to admit that I loved not going to the office. That weekend warrior mentality moved in full-time, and I found that I can't do without the added relaxation anymore. I still get my work done, but it's not about sitting at a desk anymore. It's about streamlining meetings, working from home, and being in control of my time. I can handle a distribution dispute and then go for a bike ride or shoot arrows in my backyard for a while.

The work/life balance I can achieve these days is amazing, all thanks to utilizing the available technology. Nobody in my office even knew what Zoom was a year ago, although it was already a mainstream method of videoconferencing. There was no reason to try it out before. Now we're all logged into Microsoft Teams on our phones and computers. We can do business whenever it needs to be done; the rest of the time is ours. I might be lying by the pool, but I'm still linked in with my company. I took the Zoom call about doing this very book while I was waiting for the winds to change for paragliding; I just changed my backdrop to look like an office.

I'm 100 percent dedicated to the company and my dad's legacy, but they don't have to fill 100 percent of my life; in an odd way, I owe that freedom to the advances we all underwent during a pandemic. There can be more to me than my job, and I want everyone to share in that—especially my employees. We work as a means to live the life we want and to take care of our loved ones, but if work is all you are, what's the point? Everyone needs money, sure, but you only get one shot at this life.

Over the years, I have met so many individuals who make their identity about one thing, and for a lot of people, that thing is their job. They become their job, or hobby, or distraction. People tend to seek out activities and identify as the activity rather than finding out who they really are. "I'm a lawyer, so that's all I do all day. Even when I'm out with friends, I'm just the lawyer friend." Or "I'm a skydiver, so I need to live in a van and drive to my next jump. No time for anything but that adrenaline rush, sorry."

Jobs, hobbies, distractions—those are only what people do, not who they are. I encourage the people I meet to be more than they are. Good for you for having a profession or an interest. I appreciate your passion, but you aren't a one-dimensional being. Don't miss your kid's soccer game to make it to a meeting. Reschedule and be with the ones who matter most. The meeting can wait. Don't sacrifice the important moments in your life for the sake of a job. You'll live a life of regret, which will ruin any success you might have hoped for.

I'm not suggesting you should shirk your responsibilities. You can't ignore your problems and live with your head in the sand. Get your work done when you need to and learn to prioritize what matters most to you. Galardi Group has 350 restaurants, which equate to 350 problems in a given day. Because we have franchises rather than company stores, there's only so much we can do to help those franchisees out if they're in a bind. The employees belong to the franchisees, not to Galardi; in other words, we don't control them. Every franchisee is a small business owner, and they're all looking to the person in the room with the most money to make things all better. As much as I'd like to, I can't get on the phone and tell a franchisee, "Go ahead and increase your starting wage to eighteen bucks an hour, and give out two-hundred-dollar discretionary bonuses to employees who've done a great job." It would be awesome if I could wave that magic wand and erase their problems, but they need to find solutions that work for their particular store. As I mentioned before, most of the time they just want to be heard, so we hear them out. We shoulder the blame, we weather the storm, and once everything has calmed down, we talk them through fixing what's wrong.

Following Dad's example and establishing a presence while remaining unemotional, which I've gotten better at over time, is something I do both inside and outside the office. It's been interesting to see how both of those worlds affect each other. I've learned to trust in my own judgment, a lot of which came through skydiving and other action sports that require a complete trust in oneself in order to survive. When the wind is ripping at your body, everything becomes a critical decision. If something goes wrong, you have to instantly react with the right choice or else it's going to go really, really wrong. Trusting yourself enough to take your own life in your hands and jump off a cliff or out of a plane translates into inner confidence that you can't get anywhere else. Plummeting through the sky and making it safely back to the ground makes any boardroom decision seem like a piece of cake in comparison.

That lifestyle has served me well, but I thought I'd always be a bachelor. I just never thought I'd find a girl who could keep up with me. Boy, was I wrong. As I mentioned earlier, I had gotten into competitive snowboarding and found myself at the Winter X Games in 2016, so I was twenty-seven at the time. I had a lot of friends who were more serious about the sport than I was, and many of them went on to become professional snowboarders, but I was mainly there to hang out in my hometown and just enjoy the vibe. So, on one of those days, my buddy and I were standing in the lift line and this smoking-hot girl walks up, gives my friend a hug, then turns to me and says:

"You're a terrible dancer."

What the hell? I thought. *Who is this and what do they know about my dancing?*

I stood there, struck with confusion, and my buddy filled me in. I'd done a lot more partying than snowboarding in Aspen this go-round, and the night before, I'd gotten carried away at a nightclub (I'm such a great role model, I know), and had apparently done some dancing. I recalled none of it, but he said I'd asked this girl to dance and made a fool out of myself.

"I'm Natalie," she said. "Call me Nat."

There may have been some response on my end, but I couldn't really get anything out because of how mind-blowingly gorgeous she was. She headed away and my buddy and I got onto the chairlift to head up the hill.

"Who was that?" I asked him.

"She told you, dude," he replied. "That's Nat. She's a promo model for Monster Energy."

"How do you know her?"

"We used to kinda hang out for a while. She's great."

"Can I . . . Do you mind if I talk to her?"

"No problem, man. Go for it."

I wonder what his response would have been if he knew we'd end up married.

I didn't get another chance to talk with Nat that day, but we both ended up at a big group dinner later that night, thanks to our mutual acquaintances. We spent most of the evening just talking to each other, and it was great. That night, a massive snowstorm rolled through Colorado and closed every airport in the state. That was bad news for a lot of people, what with all the flights delayed, but it couldn't have been better news for snowboarders. New snow meant a powder day, and I didn't get many powder days living in California.

Nat, myself, and two of our mutual friends hit the slopes the next morning, but I was really worried they'd drag me down or hold me back. I wanted to actually get some laps in and internally decided to uphold the old rule of "no friends on a powder day." Meaning, if they couldn't keep up, I'd see them later for lunch. The other two sucked, but suddenly Nat went blasting past me, just absolutely ripping down the hill, and I hurried to keep up. She was phenomenal, and I was starting to see that in more ways than one. Not only was she keeping pace with my every move, she was actually pushing me to go faster and try harder.

We finished our day, which was epic, and I asked her where she was living.

"Newport Beach," she said. I couldn't believe it. This had to be more than just a coincidence. That's exactly where I was living at the time, and when we both got back there, we spent a lot of time together. I called it dating, but she insisted it was just hanging out, because she didn't want to be in a relationship. I was patient with her and didn't want to push the matter, but a date's a date if one person pays, and I was the one paying.

That impulse from the slopes to try harder became the theme

of our relationship. No matter what we did together, our one rule was to never quit. Didn't matter what the obstacle was, or how bad the weather got, or how hard it was to keep going; if we started it, we finished it. Period. As long as we were doing it together, we would succeed.

We got to know each other a lot more, and she'd ask about my family and my work, but I didn't fill her in on a lot of the details because I was worried about how she'd react—I wanted her to like me for me. For a long time, Nat thought I was just the guy who cooked hot dogs and set up the tents at conventions, and I let her think that because I found it hilarious. The fact that she thought I was on the bottom rung and still gave me the time of day says a lot about her. Then I brought her to the family ranch in Aspen and had the immense pleasure of watching her entire view of me change in an instant.

She still took some convincing, but eventually, she came around. We dated for three and a half years, during which time I fell in love with her. I said to myself, *I'm going to marry this girl.* I started looking for ways to propose.

An opportunity came up in the form of a trip to Egypt that involved flying over the pyramids in wingsuits. In case you don't know what a wingsuit is, it's a big, stupid-looking suit that you put on (completely ridiculous to look at) and then you jump out of a plane or off a cliff, and it allows you to move further forward than down. So you basically become a really inefficient bird, but it's fun. Anyway, we got the opportunity to go wingsuit over the pyramids, and in my head, I thought something like:

Wow, this is going to be the best proposal ever. We'll wingsuit over one of the Seven Wonders of the World and land on one of those majestic sand dunes without a soul in sight. The sun will just be setting and we'll come in to land, and the reflection of the sunset will bounce off the pyramids and onto our faces. Breathtaking! I'll get down on one knee and give a long, drawn-out speech about how much I love this girl and why I want to spend the rest of my life with her. She'll cry and shout "Yes!" so loudly it echoes, and it's just going to be the most romantic moment in the history of the world. It's perfect!

There were a few things I failed to take into consideration. The first was that I never stopped to think about how Nat might want to be proposed to. I had this aggrandized version of how it would go in my mind, but it was all about the spectacle and it was all wrong.

The second thing I failed to consider was the logistics of pulling everything off. We flew in the night before, which was a horrible idea due to the jet lag, and had to get up at 3:30 in the morning to get on a bus, which took us on a two-hour drive to a military base. The bus was hot and smelly, basically the opposite of romantic, but Nat was still excited. She had no idea I'd snuck the ring into my bag for the big proposal. We got to the base and were rushed straight to the staging room. We were the only Americans in sight and the place only had one bathroom, which made for some cramped quarters first thing in the morning.

We got on the plane, one of these big C-130 aircrafts, and it's hot and loud. Again, the least romantic it could have been. We flew for fifteen minutes and reached the pyramids, and suddenly it was time to jump. Out of the plane we went and took off through the sky. That part was beautiful, so I start patting myself on the back about how flawless my plan was. We'd be engaged in no time flat.

Then I look down and realize we aren't going to land on a majestic sand dune. We're heading straight for a gravel parking lot that's absolutely *packed* with people. Not just the usual tourists, but huge crowds pouring out of buses and news vans. We pull our chutes and I see that we'll have to land directly in the middle of everyone. It's the only clear space.

See, my third mistake was that I'd told a buddy what I had planned. He was supposed to be the only one who knew, but he'd told a friend, who told a friend, who alerted the Egyptian media that something big was going down.

It takes me a minute to figure out that all these people are reporters and camera crews. This guy with a huge TV camera points and just starts sprinting straight at me, but trips and falls on his face right in the gravel. The guy behind him, who I think was the news anchor, doesn't skip a beat and *hurdles* his camera man (without even checking on him) to make sure he gets a spot at the front as we land.

We get swarmed by a hundred faces, all poking cameras and microphones at us and absolutely blasting us with questions. I think to myself, *This is the worst idea ever. Nat would hate everything about this as a proposal.*

But, like an idiot, I didn't want to lose the opportunity and decided to press on. I called her over in front of all the cameras, which she took in stride because the jump she'd just made was actually historic. She was the first woman to ever wingsuit over the pyramids in Egypt. The first ever! In hindsight, I'm kicking myself for not stopping everything and just letting her savor her moment. It was such a huge deal, but did I let that deter me from what I saw as the perfect moment?

Nope.

"Nat," I said, and I went down on one knee as the media snapped pictures and recorded the whole thing. The look of confusion on her face was so priceless and so justified. I whipped out the ring I'd been hiding and shoved it right up in her face and shouted, "I love you!"

And that was it. Overwhelmed with the moment, I had closed my eyes in anticipation, but when I opened them again, I could tell she wasn't happy with me. There are people who like surprises, and then there's Natalie. I hadn't spoken a word of this to her, we were surrounded by strangers, it was terribly unromantic, and on top of all that, I'd completely bulldozed over her big accomplishment.

Everyone in the crowd starts shouting, "Kiss him! Kiss him!" and "Say yes! Do it!" There's cheering and smiling, a few people are hugging, even the classic old woman wiping tears from her eyes. With all that going on, Nat's working through a jumble of emotions and could probably see the realization dawning on my face as my grin slipped.

"Oh, mmaaAaaYybee?" she said with a little shrug. With all the noise, I'm not sure if the cameras picked up what she said, but I heard her loud and clear. There were a dozen layers to her response, and we got a chance to unwrap them all with some spirited discussion on our way out of the parking lot as the crowd dispersed. Suffice it to say, I had learned an important lesson about what *not* to do.

However, that was just day one of our trip. We still had three more days of wingsuiting around the pyramids, and I had plenty to think about.

So the next day, we did a jump and came in to land, and this girl came rushing over and asked to take a photo with us. I thought to myself, *She just watched us jump over the pyramids, so she must want a picture of that.* She snapped the shot and then said, "Wow, thanks. You guys are the most famous people in Egypt right now."

Nat and I looked at each other, not comprehending what the girl had just said.

"Yeah," she continued, "your proposal yesterday is on the cover of every newspaper. It's the headlining news story on every TV station."

We didn't believe her, so she brought up a video on her phone. There I was on the screen, kneeling down in front of Nat. It had maybe been twenty-four hours since that happened. There were over eight million views.

Now, anyone who has ever proposed knows how intimidating it can be, how nervous you can get, and how much effort it takes to make that leap. You're worried it will go wrong, that they'll say no, or laugh in your face, or any one of a million other things that go into the equation. Imagine being shot down in front of a hundred strangers. Then imagine eight million other strangers watching the recording of your failure and leaving likes, commenting, sharing, etc. To say it's embarrassing is an understatement.

For the next couple of days, I tried to fend off reporters and dodge interviews while that one mistaken moment sort of compounded between me and Nat. We essentially agreed to pretend it hadn't happened, but it had. Eventually, we got on a plane and came back to the US, where Egyptian media doesn't really hold any sway.

We dated for a while longer, but that whole encounter just became too much, and we broke up. I told myself that it was fine, that it was understandable, and that life would move on in a different direction. What's another breakup? I'd find somebody else, right?

We went our separate ways but stayed in touch. Actually, we talked to each other a lot more than most exes do. Nat called me at 6:30 a.m. every morning to chat, which was always a bright point in my day. Still, we weren't together and dated other people as time went by, but after eight months of being broken up, Nat suddenly said, "We should get married." It was so out of the blue that I just hung up on her. I was at the gym and went straight back to my workout, unsure what to think about what had just happened. But as my heart raced and my thoughts aligned, I realized something important: you need to understand what else is out there to know what you have.

I knew what else was out there, and I knew it wasn't what I wanted. I wanted Nat. I decided to try to repropose to her, this time—hopefully—the right way.

I asked her to come to my house in San Clemente. When she walked in, I had music playing from her favorite band, the Lumineers, and I was kneeling at the top of the stairs. Surrounding us were three replica pyramids, which I'd bought in Egypt and set up to redeem myself from the first failed pyramid. As the song ended, I stood up, wrapped my arms around her, and asked, "Will you marry me?"

With tears in her eyes, she said yes. It was one of those absolutely perfect moments, intimate and romantic, without flash photography and a hundred strangers pointing and shouting, and suddenly we were engaged. We both knew we'd made the right choice.

We started planning the wedding right away. I was in the process of selling my beautiful ranch in Colorado, but we decided we wanted to get married there before the sale finalized. We scheduled the wedding for December 7, 2019, and planned the entire thing in just two weeks. Once the plans were made, we went to Europe for a month to BASE jump and enjoy each other's company. Right after we got back from our trip, we got married.

After the wedding, it occurred to me that the date we got married was exactly one year from the day I proposed in Egypt. One of my biggest failures had become my greatest success.

We couldn't be a more perfect match. We have all the big stuff in common, like life goals and mindset, but also small stuff, like we both get super excited over the same knickknacks we find. We found these rusted metal dinosaur yard statues that are just awesome and put them all around our house. Our house now looks like Jurassic Park. Maybe love is all about tchotchkes.

She's a huge part of my life. I tell her about what's going on in my world or go to her with my work stresses, and she always steers me straight, especially when it comes to dealing with people.

"I've got to let Jane go," I'll say.

"Are you sure?" she'll reply. "I think she's wonderful. Can't you keep her, or use her somewhere else?"

Nat is unmatched when it comes to reading people. She can meet someone who works with me and get a feel for them right away: "This guy sucks. He needs to go."

Ten times out of ten, her instincts were completely accurate. Somewhere down the line, her impression, which she gave me weeks or even months back, proves itself to be true, and the person she had a bad feeling about ends up fired because they've been slacking on the job, or can't make their deadlines, or just aren't a good fit anymore. And Nat knew it the first two minutes talking to them.

We all hear how important it is to find a partner who really gets you, who you can grow with; it will show in every aspect of your life, and it couldn't have been more evident to me than with Nat. She and I share a lot of interests and we both like to be active. We've built a lot of our relationship doing adventure sports, like skydiving, BASE jumping, paragliding, dirt biking, and of course, snowboarding. Though we love them all, it's hard to relax when your adrenaline is pumping, and no one can stay in that state for long.

I've learned the importance of having something to do that

is equally satisfying as it is therapeutic and relaxing. To unwind and destress, I have to do things that take focus while my body is still. Something like sitting in a hot tub, or building something in the garage, or playing the piano. If you had told me when I was eight that I play the piano to relax and wind down, I'd have called you a liar. As a kid, I learned to play the piano, and I hated it so much. I was the classic grumpy child, sitting sullenly on the bench with my arms crossed, just wishing I could get away and go play outside. Mom saw my struggle and told me that I could quit piano lessons if I'd learn how to play one full song. So I learned the song as quickly as I could, then quit. For a long time, music took a backseat to all my other interests, which all seemed to involve falling down. Extreme sports take a toll on your body; I've broken twenty-three bones at this point in my life.

During one of my recoveries from those broken bones, I decided to pick up piano playing again, and this time around, something clicked. My interest in piano spread quickly to other instruments. I started getting into music more and more, all genres, and I found an interest in being a deejay. I produced my own music and used to deejay weddings. By the time I went through my gen. ed. courses at the University of Colorado, I realized I didn't enjoy much of college beyond my music classes. So I decided to pursue a degree in music and settled on a music business major with a minor in piano.

Upon starting my courses, I learned really quickly that not all people have an innate knack for music, and I was one of the ones who didn't. Without some of the raw talent or innate skills that others were seemingly born with, I found I had to work ten times harder to keep up. Around me, there were classmates with perfect pitch. That meant they could hear a B flat and be able to say, without a doubt, "That's a B flat." There are people known as synesthetes who see colors when they hear sounds, so one piece of music might "look purple" to them, and I had several of them in my program. Rather than simply listening to music, they could see it and feel it. Other students could listen to a piano concerto and write the notes down as it played. It was like something out of *X-Men*. I had no hope of competing with that level of skill; it wasn't part of my sperm lottery. Nonetheless, just because I wasn't naturally the most adept at music didn't mean it couldn't be an important aspect of who I am holistically.

I had learned in other aspects of life to put my strengths where they could be most useful within the context of my passion for music. I could do the business side of music, and that's what led me to my position as a concert promoter. I didn't see rainbows or chromatic scales, but I did see costs, profits, liabilities, and assets, so I played to my strengths. And that's what it comes down to . . . play your strengths—and encourage others to do the same—and surround yourself with people and environments that encourage you to grow and shift with the changing tides.

JR and Natalie on their wedding day at the Galardi family ranch in Aspen, Colorado, 2019.

Celebrating Natalie's birthday on Paradise Island in The Bahamas, 2021.

Natalie wingsuiting over the pyramids in Egypt. (photo taken by JR, flying above her)

Mindset

16

I am the type of person who enjoys being underestimated. I prefer being the withdrawn dark horse, because when someone has a preconceived notion of who you are and what you're capable of, you're the one who's in control of choosing when to surprise them. Their assumptions work in your favor. I can't count how many times I've walked into a meeting and someone said, "Oh, good, the kid's here to set up the projector," or gave me their coffee order, or let me know what they wanted for lunch, only to see the looks on their faces change to shock when they found out who I really was. There's power in being under the radar. Whether I learned that from Dad or not, I can't say; it's just how I approach first impressions.

"Dress for the job you want, not the job you have," is not a generalized label that should be equally applied to everyone.

Naturally, a lot of people in business wear the corporate suits and cufflinks, have the trimmed and clean-cut look, and want to just exude that air of professionalism. My father was one of them. While there's nothing wrong with that, I have more on my mind than how I look. That's not to say I'm a slob, because I clean up nicely when I need to, but I like my hair longer, I've got some tattoos, and I like to keep some facial hair. I don't shave religiously, so you might catch me looking scruffy depending on the day, but who cares? I'm more than my appearance, and so are you. There's more to us than the clothes we have on, or our haircuts, or any other physical traits I could name. I'm not a pair of cufflinks, and I'm not a t-shirt and jeans. I may not always look polished, but what can I do? What can I bring to the table despite my baseball cap? I enjoy earning the respect of others through what I have to say, and by taking action to prove my value.

While I understand that I'm in a position where I can easily designate what I wear as "office appropriate," the bigger picture I'm getting at here is that we've been conditioned to associate certain costumes with certain intelligence, and that isn't accurate. It's a lesson woven into me by my parents and the education they provided. It is equally important to understand that a well-dressed imposter can do just as much, if not more, harm than someone in rags.

Never once have I stopped, looked around the room, and thought, *I'm the richest guy in here.* That isn't something that crosses my mind, ever. In fact, I only know to mention it in this context because it's apparently on a lot of other people's minds. I get asked to invest in everything under the sun. I get the elevator pitches, the nightclub pitches, the walk-you-to-your-car pitches. "Great opportunity for you to get in on the ground floor! I just need X amount of dollars to get it started." None of these people are looking to share in an investment, and they don't think I can add valuable information to their potential business; they just want money, and that is all they see me as. What they don't realize is that I only invest in my own business at this point. I invest in myself. When it comes down to it, no matter how much money you have in your bank account or how many plates you're successfully spinning at once, the only thing you really own at the end of the day is yourself.

Being judged as a walking dollar sign was an adjustment for me. When I was growing up in Colorado, everyone around me took me at face value. To them, I was just a laid-back kid hanging out with other laid-back kids. Meeting someone new meant I got asked my name, what I liked to do, what school I went to, who else I knew, etc. Even later as an adult, the questions were largely the same. They just wanted to get to know me for who I was.

Upon moving to LA, one of the first things I noticed was how people introduced themselves. They wanted to know how I earned money.

"What's your name?"

"JR."

"Great, great. What do you do?"

"Tons of stuff. I'm into archery and skydiving and—"

"No, no. What do you do for a living?"

"Oh, I run a business."

"Good stuff. What kinda numbers are you pulling down?"

It seems harmless enough, unless you know better. It is uncouth to ask someone how much money they make upon initially meeting them, regardless of their profession. Line by line, the aforementioned conversation is usually the extent of it all, unless they feel like making an investment pitch. I've had this encounter more times than I can remember, and it gets stale pretty fast. The kind of people who approach me like this are just trying to assess my status, my importance, all based on a dollar amount. They value your perceived monetary worth, not your worth as a person. What an overwhelming disappointment. All these ulterior motives have developed into such an irritating trend that now, I'm actually surprised when someone doesn't ask me for money. I hate that this has become my expectation these days. It's a surefire way to get walled off from me. Nonetheless, it comes with the territory of who I am.

My dad's legacy was handed to me, gift-wrapped in gold and glowing with promise. I have never wanted to hide from that fact. I consider it my responsibility to preserve that legacy and find ways to improve upon it. At the same time that I've been entrusted with my father's past, I have to create my own future. This is the driving factor behind everything I do. Some might consider that to be a lot of pressure, but I don't see it that way. Although I felt a huge amount of pressure in the beginning, that's all behind me now. I don't worry that what I'm doing is sufficient anymore; I know it is, and that confidence comes with experience.

Learning to trust one's own judgement happens at different intervals in life for different people—but the one thing it has in common for us all is that it takes time and it takes experiences. There's no other way around it. In my early twenties, my go-to mindset was to just pretend I knew what I was doing: feigned confidence. Some people say, "Fake it till you make it," and that's exactly what I did until I had a better internal gauge for my discernment. Internally, I was a mess of doubt and confusion because I knew that one wrong choice could be disastrous, and I didn't have enough experience to recognize a wrong choice ahead of time. When Dad passed away, I just sat there and thought, *Oh God, this is all on me now. No one else is going to take the steps necessary to keep the wheels turning. All of my family—and all the families of the franchisees, all the executives and their families—depend on these paychecks. If I don't step up, or if I screw this up, everything falls apart.*

I was being a touch overly dramatic, as the company runs very well, but without me in the picture, there would be no more family business. Someone else would have stepped in and bought it out, and everything under Galardi Group would be very different now, assuming it existed at all.

Yet, that fear of failure that brought out my imposter syndrome also drove me to set goals for myself, and nothing ever really gets done without a goal attached. Even in the face of something unknown, like a pandemic, goals keep us moving forward without getting bogged down in worry and despair. It was difficult to maintain goals as a business during COVID, because every day seemed like a new way to panic, but we kept our heads on straight and didn't lose sight of building the brand. Thanks to our drive-thrus, we could stay open, but we didn't just high-five each other for John Galardi's innovative thinking, sit back, and watch. We shifted our marketing to match the trend, which meant focusing more on customer retention than new customer acquisition. Now that things have settled somewhat, we can look into expanding elsewhere. We recently started an international branch of the Galardi Group and registered our trademark and name in seventeen different countries. We're in talks with franchisees in each of those countries to set up shop very soon, which will make Wienerschnitzel an international brand. It's incredibly exciting for us.

Shifting our focus required us to hire a director of international franchising, who already had an existing network overseas for companies like Burger King, Carl's Jr., and Sbarro's. The best part about the foreign franchises is that they're almost exclusively owned by two or three people, so that really streamlines how we can do business with them. They know what they want, and it's not another burger concept, or pizza, or pasta. Nobody has a hot dog concept, so that's where we come in. We're making the move to an international level, and it's all because we set a company goal. It wouldn't have happened otherwise.

For my personal goals, my drive is to always become a better version of myself, which may not necessarily coincide with how others perceive me—and certain better versions of myself might not be visible to the outside observer. I never want to make an improvement to myself just because someone else expects it. Improvement should come from within; otherwise it simply won't be authentic, and it will fail.

I make it a point to seek out ways to improve myself from every given angle. Physical fitness has obviously been a major part of my life, so I seek new ways to learn physically, work my mental and physical strength in new ways, and test my limits.

I consider self-defense to be a necessity for everyone, so I'm currently training in Jiu-Jitsu. It's more widely known these days, but nobody knew about it for a while; now you can find gyms all over. There's an instinctual response aspect to it that I absolutely love, and it meshes well with my background in extreme sports to help me react fully and forcefully at the right moment. Maybe I'll need it walking down the street and maybe I won't, but you could say I've learned the importance of being ready for a fight after that friendly, drunken boxing match in the garage.

Intellectual pursuits are equally as crucial for me, so Nat and I study and learn about new things all the time. Lately, I have been very into physics, so we both picked out a pile of books and just went through them together. We ask each other questions, share our thoughts, and build our knowledge one page at a time, side by side. It's all about expanding our minds beyond what they were yesterday, but it doesn't all have to be dusty tomes and scientific papers.

I make it a goal to read—only now instead of earning tangible coins for my pages, I understand each page is actually an investment in enriching my mind. I'm currently reading *100*

Deadly Skills by Clint Emerson, and it's awesome. He teaches ways to get out of intense situations using improvisation and awareness, so there are sections about escaping from duct tape restraints and zip ties, or how to make a concealed-carry pistol holster out of a coat hanger. There's also a *Survival Edition* that goes through outdoor survival training, which suits my taste for extreme sports, and a *Combat Edition* that covers topics like disarming a gunman and otherwise filling your "badass" toolbox. They're such a blast to read through.

It is equally important to find something you enjoy with childlike wonderment as it is to do something considered classically "intellectually stimulating." Nat and I share equal enthusiasm for aliens. If you haven't had a chance to watch *Ancient Aliens* on History Channel, do yourself a favor and go blow your mind. My god, they're up to seventeen seasons now, and you just binge watch the entire thing. It's not so much about believing it as truth as it is an exercise in thinking outside the box. I'm not typically one for conspiracies and supernatural stuff (unlike Nat), but that show will shake you up! By the way, on the off chance there are some extraterrestrials reading this right now, let me know if you're interested in a Wienerschnitzel franchise on Mars or wherever. I'd love to do a UFO Dog sometime.

I think everyone should try to constantly learn something from those around them. We've all heard the saying that you're a product of the five people you interact with the most, and in my opinion, that's absolutely the truth. There's another saying that's been attributed to everyone from Confucius to Lorne Michaels that goes, "If you're the smartest person in the room, you're in the wrong room." Adages like these might seem corny or trite at first glance, but they really hold so much wisdom if we'll just listen. Fundamentally, there's truth to it or it wouldn't have persisted throughout history, across cultures. I encourage you to stop and take a look at who you choose to surround yourself with. That friend who's always late directly impacts you. The buddy who tells inappropriate jokes in public rubs off on you. Don't get distracted by just the negative stuff, however, because what you should be looking for are the positive attributes that subtly transform who you are.

Although I have had no shortage of experiences with influential people in my life, my primary source of influence has always been my dad. He came from abject poverty and, through sheer work ethic and drive, built a huge company that affects hundreds of millions of people. The way he comported himself, his bearing, his demeanor, are all qualities that I respect so much. His memory motivates me, but as the majority of the content of this book is directly about his influence on my life, there are two others who I would be remiss to leave out: Mom and Nat.

I admire my mom so much. She came from an incredibly abusive household, and she didn't transfer one iota of that upbringing to me. She used to collect cans and trade them for money to eat, but she always had dinner on the table for her family. When she started with the company, not only was she a fish out of water who had to deal with an overwhelming amount of stress, she had to put up with her own son pitted against her. I wasn't easy to deal with, I'm sure. I suppose I've never been easy to deal with when it comes to my mom, but those first few years after Dad passed, I really put her through the wringer. It wasn't until much later that she told me those were the hardest years of her life. I wish I could go back and do things differently, but I was a grieving twenty-three-year-old, and I took it out on her. She is resilient, however, and has persevered through so many struggles, and we've made it a goal to constantly work on our relationship and make up for lost time. I'd say things are better between us now than they ever have been.

My mom is cut from a completely different cloth; you've just got to see her in action to understand. Go check out her episode of *Undercover Boss* sometime. No matter what she does, she goes all-in and doesn't let anything get in her way. Although she is in her seventies, you would never guess for an instant that age had any impact on her. She decided to get into competitive fitness and ended up placing in contest after contest. Car racing drew her interest, so off she went to do that. Just picture a seventy-year-old woman blasting around a race track and totally killing it, because that's what she does. Her schedule these days starts with Pilates first thing in the morning, then weightlifting, then she goes horseback riding before heading to her responsibilities as CEO.

My mother's fearlessness astounds me. I decided at some point to go get my AFF (Accelerated Free Fall) license, and guess who wanted to go along? Watching my own mother jump out of a plane at 10,000 feet was a singular experience, and she didn't just go once. On her second jump, she had a cut-away, which means that her original parachute malfunctioned with a line twist and she had to cut it away to make room for her reserve chute. It's incredibly scary. Seasoned skydivers can do 500 jumps and never have a cut-away. She performed the maneuver, but she held onto her main chute and ended up crash-landing on the runway, where she popped right back up and wanted to go again.

To say that she's special is a massive understatement, and I will always be proud to be her son.

I have reserved my final recognition for the person closest to me, who influences me, drives me, and helps motivate me to be that better version of myself: my wife, Natalie. I've never met anyone so unapologetically herself. She is who she is, and she doesn't need anyone's approval on the matter. I tend to be conflict-averse, which is to say I keep my opinions to myself; Nat doesn't have that trait. She speaks her mind at all times, and I love that about her. It's admirable, because she likes herself, and I don't know that a lot of people can honestly say the same. This might translate to arrogance in someone else, but Nat tempers her confidence with genuine care and concern for others, and she sees people with a clarity that few can emulate.

Nat has this uncanny ability to see the truth about situations sooner than others do. Her personal reading led her into research about intelligence levels in pigs, which led her into how pigs are treated in the food industry. The facts are unpleasant, so she came to me and said, "These methods are cruel. What would it take for you to remove pork from the restaurants?" Recognizing one of

Nat's hunches, I met with my team to discuss eliminating all pork from our menu. We're currently in the process of doing exactly what she recommended, and it turns out the timing couldn't have been better. Thanks to Nat, my purchasing department thinks I'm a damn genius because the price of pork is rising drastically. New propositions regarding humanely farming pigs have recently come into effect, calling for more space between pigs and better care. More space means fewer pigs per farm, and fewer pigs means less quantity and higher prices. The market for pork is about to skyrocket, and we're already about six months ahead of everybody else, all because of my amazing wife.

Influential people are worthless to you if you don't implement the lessons you've learned from them in your life. I can have all the good influences in the world, but if I don't actually use what I've learned from them, then why did I spend my time with them? Why did I waste their time?

One of my biggest habits, my daily schedule, is something I developed by taking note of the habits of my role models, those who influenced me, and putting them into something I can utilize for my own personal growth. At some point, we all must choose to take action to progress ourselves, and for me, that meant creating a daily plan that allows me to reach my full potential.

I've tailored each aspect of my schedule to supplement my productivity each day.

Mornings are critical to my success, and my schedule usually doesn't change for that first part of the day. My alarm goes off at 4:45 a.m., but it's not a death knell the way some people view it.

It's a personal choice that I made for myself. I've known too many people who've struggled through much harder things than me, who still had to get up and get to work, so I don't consider it my prerogative to complain. I don't dread the signal to begin kicking ass. To me, the alarm says, "You may begin."

The first thing I do when I wake up is exercise; that's the time when my body is at its most rested and when I feel like I get my best results. In my opinion, this step is non-negotiable, because it gives me a motivational surge of energy that carries me through the entire day. I've always tried to keep my body in shape because of the sports and activities I'm into, but exercise is also an investment in myself. It doesn't matter how successful I am in life; if I don't take care of my health, I won't be around long enough to enjoy my accomplishments.

After the workout is a shower, which I use to orient my mind on the day's necessities. Not a line-by-line layout, necessarily, but an overview of what's expected of me and what I expect from myself. It could be considered meditation in a formal sense, but I view it more as a conversation with the inner me. This is where I set and refocus my goals, check in on my progress, and remind myself what I'm working toward in the big picture. As an added bonus, I'm clean for the day.

I don't do pep talks in the mirror. Having a mantra can be helpful for some people, but I have never seen a benefit, personally. Instead, I find myself driven by the urge to prove myself. I'm the founder's son, but I never want anyone to believe I'm undeserving of what I've been given. I don't want to be caught slipping, so that constantly pushes me forward to do more and be better. Personal reading helps educate me, and I spend at least an hour each morning reading new books and learning new things alongside my wife. The topics can be scattershot, but I'm a firm believer that any type of knowledge builds my mind.

Expand your perception of what an "influential person" means to you. Think beyond money, power, and position. Oftentimes, you don't have to seek people outside of those closest to you to learn. Nat came to me one day and said she'd read about the benefits of celery juice. "We need it!" she told me. "We have to drink it every day!" She went on about the health benefits, how it clears up your skin, detoxifies your liver, and fights all these types of cancer, and she just had all this overwhelming evidence of how amazing it was to cure all our problems. So we gave it a shot; got the juicer, got the celery, made the juice. What the studies didn't say was how incredibly rough this stuff is on your stomach. It clears you out, definitely, but it also gives you the worst case of flatulence you've ever experienced, like, for hours.

Successful people, influential people, come in all shapes, sizes, ethnicities, and backgrounds, and I have been privileged to have met so many successful people in my life. Some of them aren't good people internally, and that kind won't last in the long run, because nobody wants to work for or with terrible people for long. But the vast majority of successful people I've encountered are wonderful, and that group—the ones who will last—all possess one trait in particular: humility. They're able to put others before themselves, and they work hard without the need for recognition. Those who are humbly successful get up and grind without waiting to be told they're doing a good job.

I make it a point to model my actions after the people I admire. That means sacrifice and dedication, which can look different to different people. Because I have chosen to work in a business that I am passionate about, that is in my blood, that is a part of who I am, there are no days off for me. I just don't feel like taking days off; it's not something I want to do. If you have work to do, you get up, you shower, and you get the job done no matter what—it won't be a problem for you if you're passionate about what you're doing. If you're shaking your head while reading this, saying to yourself, "Easy for you to say; you're the president of your father's company," then I deeply encourage you to begin exploring what you can do as a career that incorporates your passion and allows your dedication to come organically. There's no one-size-fits-all, and it takes trial and error, but when you find what you're meant to be doing, the concept of no days off isn't just some weird flex to tell others how hard you hustle; it feels natural because you enjoy what you're doing.

Your perspective of your personal time influences how you perceive your purpose. There is no perfect day. There is no terrible day. You're mistaken if you believe that your circumstances are at the mercy of good and bad days, because you are the one who controls the outcome at all times. You yourself might have ups and downs, but learn to recognize that your success, or lack thereof, is the direct result of what's going on inside your head.

JR Galardi flying over the North Shore of Hawaii.
#worklifebalance

Advising the Future

17

None of us can change the past. We can decide our present and affect our future, but what's done is done. If yesterday was unsatisfactory, it's already locked in; the only thing we can do is learn from it and move on.

What I've learned from my own past is that I should have acted sooner on so many things. All the changes I've implemented over the years—the improvements and promotions and rearranging—would have been so much more beneficial if they'd happened earlier. One particular thing I wish I had begun immediately is philanthropy work. We should have pulled the trigger on it the instant we had the resources. I think about all the people we could have helped, and that just serves to drive me even harder to help people now. I don't want to miss another opportunity.

Other changes aren't as important, but they still would have served to boost productivity for the company, which would have equated to more money. And it's not how much money you have, but what you do with it that counts, remember? Selling more food means helping more people.

A couple years ago, we put in holding units for hamburgers into all of our Wienerschnitzel restaurants. I was concerned about them at first, because we're a cook-to-order establishment, which means the order comes in and we cook your food right away so it's always fresh. But we weren't moving enough people through and those orders were slowing us down, causing us to lose customers. Burgers take a long time to make, and that slows down the flow of the entire kitchen. So we installed the holding units that allowed the workers to precook five or ten burgers at a time and store them for up to thirty minutes. As it turns out, the burgers heated in the cooker and went through a sort of marinating stage, which made them even better than fresh off the grill. People loved them. This one little step changed us from a cook-to-order restaurant to a build-to-order restaurant, and our throughput and sales jumped substantially. Seems simple in retrospect, but that old regime wouldn't have considered such a possibility: people always resist change until it becomes normalized.

Business is fickle. One bad hot dog could ruin everything, so we have to be overly cautious and vigilant about our entire process. But, the fact of the matter is that everyone needs to eat, and most of us (at least in the US) have been conditioned to eat three times a day. My dad had a saying that went something like, "Wienerschnitzel doesn't have a direct hot dog competitor, so we're not up against that problem. What we're competing for is a share of the stomach. I just want a little slice of that pie." He envisioned a customer's stomach as a pie chart, which is way more applicable than it might seem at first. There are so many options for food out there today, but there's only so much food a person can eat in a given day. Every time you choose to eat a hot dog is one less time you could have eaten a burger, or pizza, or tacos. The object of the game is to get you to choose my product over anyone else's.

My hope is that Wienerschnitzel will continue to be a family-run business, but I honestly can't say what the future holds. I don't have any children at this time, but what if someday down the line my kids have no interest in the company? What if I have a son who's exactly like me and wants to pursue his own hobbies and ventures? I don't want to force his hand, but I also don't want him to be adrift in life. I'll expect him to be up and doing things, and it won't matter what they are, as long as he's not laying around. Just in case he grows up and suddenly changes his mind, I'll make sure to teach him what I know, but I won't want to be overt about it so he doesn't feel stifled. I'll have to be subtle and take the patient approach. Business can be intimidating, and I won't want to scare him off, so I'll probably keep certain aspects of my work hidden from him until the time feels right. He might not know everything about me until he's ready to understand.

Nat will spoil the hell out of our kids, and that's a fact. She will absolutely be the one paying our children to go to time out, but I know the long-term effects of that method and might pay a quarter here and there myself. It worked for me.

If I were to impart any advice to my children and grandchildren, it would be to refrain from judging anyone by their financial situation. Bank accounts don't matter. Don't ask people what they do for a living until you've learned something about who they are. Jobs aren't personality attributes. Be as ready to make friends as two little boys in the middle of a festival. Learn to speak the language of friendship. Surround yourself with people who make you better every day.

When you're old enough to make your own way, stop whatever it is you're doing and go out in the world to see what it has to offer. Get outside of your bubble and be around people who have different needs, beliefs, and aspirations than what you've known. Cross borders, find other cultures, and keep an open mind. Look around yourself and see that it's not all about you.

I realize not everyone can just drop everything and fly around the planet, especially with lockdowns and breakthrough cases and a tight economy, but consider it an investment rather than an expense. I'd go so far as to say, if you're forced to choose between going to college or traveling, skip the school and get a plane ticket, because the travel will serve you better in the long run. Diplomas are great, but they're no match for experiencing firsthand what the world has to offer.

Once you've done some traveling and gained some perspective, come back and refocus on your aspirations. Be confident in yourself and your decision-making abilities. You're going to make mistakes, but they should never prevent you from trying again.

You know more than you think you do, and the best trait you can have is adaptability. Roll with the punches and learn from everyone around you. Lean on your team, because they're your family. Make a habit of trusting people, but make certain they're worthy of that trust. Don't be afraid to call out bullshit when you see it.

Never stop rising. There's always room for growth. Expose yourself to new information every day and find ways to keep it entertaining. Challenge yourself to do surprising things and find someone to share in what you've discovered.

When my dad died, so many people said such wonderful things about him and had so many, many amazing stories to share; their memories of him were so powerful that it was almost like he wasn't gone. Almost. But I wish they'd told me more about him before he passed. No one really tells you stories about your dad while he's alive, and that's a shame. I learned so much about John Galardi after it was too late to talk to him about everything. I missed out on so many conversations I should have had.

When my time comes, what will people remember about me? Will I be known for a calm and commanding presence like he was? Will my name leave such an impact as his? I can't say for certain, but if they say half as much about me as they did about my father, I'll be honored. The biggest compliment I've received came after a big meeting involving many of the same people who worked alongside my dad for many years; the pressure was on, so I'd handled some business and given my input. Afterward, several company members approached me, and they all said,

"You are your father's son." That really let me know I was on the right track.

All I can hope for is that I'll be seen as someone who didn't waste an opportunity. I was handed a legacy, and I won't squander it or coast along. Everything I do is geared toward taking my father's dream and making it even bigger and better.

I can't wait to see where we'll be in another sixty years.

"I am one of the lucky ones to have been able to work with both John and JR. They're amazing leaders and I would do anything for them (as would anyone else who worked with them over the years). What makes everyone so loyal is that they've always shown their loyalty to us first. From the first time you meet them, they treat franchisees, employees, and vendors like family. They genuinely care about others and I thank them for allowing me to have a blessed life being part of the Galardi Group family."

- Doug Koegeboehn
Chief Marketing Officer of The Galardi Group

AFTERWORD

After the first draft of this book, the following email was sent out by then-executive chairperson Cindy Culpepper to all of the Galardi Group employees and Wienerschnitzel franchisees . . .

MEMORANDUM

From: CINDY CULPEPPER, EXECUTIVE CHAIRPERSON
To: ALL GALARDI GROUP EMPLOYEES
Date: JANUARY 27, 2022
Re: PROMOTION - JR GALARDI

I am pleased to announce the promotion of JR Galardi to the position of Chief Executive Officer; he will be responsible for the day-to-day operations of the company, strategy execution, and meeting our shared goals. I will retain my position as Executive Chairperson of the board and ensure we put the welfare of our franchisees and employees first.

This change is effective February 1st.

Congratulations to JR.

Cindy Culpepper, Executive Chairperson

ABOUT THE AUTHORS

JOHN GALARDI

John Galardi was the founder of Galardi Group, the parent company of Wienerschnitzel, The Original Hamburger Stand, and Tastee-Freez. He was a man of humble beginnings who grew up in Kansas City, Missouri, then moved to California at the age of nineteen. Within three days, he landed his first job working for Glen Bell Jr. at a Taco Tia restaurant, where he found his passion for business. John opened the first Wienerschnitzel in 1961 at the young age of twenty-three, and could be found working the kitchen, at the register, chatting with guests, and even going door to door to attract new customers. While growing his brand, John built a team of talented professionals who were all dedicated to his vision and the future of the company. His entrepreneurial spirit and tireless work resulted in profound success for him and his family.

JR GALARDI

As the son of Wienerschnitzel founder John Galardi, JR started in the business when he was thirteen. Working the fry station, cashier, and janitorial duties during summers throughout high school, he interned as a Wienerschnitzel Franchise Business Consultant during college to gain valuable experience in how to support the company's franchisees. After graduating from the University of Colorado, JR worked as a marketing manager and confronted a key topic regarding the future of Wienerschnitzel: How do we attract the next generation of customers? His answer to this was the Visionary marketing team, created to hit the streets and meet the younger generation face to face. Over the years, the Visionary "activation" team has served millions of free hot dogs and attracted new Wienerschnitzel guests through unique channels of public service, social media, concerts, and other special events, plus strategic integration with extreme athlete sponsorships. JR has held positions as Director of Administration, Executive Vice President, and is now President and CEO of Galardi Group, Inc. JR is the face of the future, active in developing new partnerships and bringing innovative and profitable solutions to the ever-growing Wienerschnitzel family.

ABOUT THE PUBLISHER

Di Angelo Publications was founded in 2008 by Sequoia Schmidt—at the age of seventeen. The modernized publishing firm's creative headquarters is in Houston, Texas, with its distribution center located in Twin Falls, Idaho. The subsidiary rights department is based in Los Angeles, and Di Angelo Publications has recently grown to include branches in England, Australia, and Sequoia's home country of New Zealand. In 2020, Di Angelo Publications made a conscious decision to move all printing and production for domestic distribution of its books to the United States. The firm is comprised of eleven imprints, and the featured imprint, Aspire, was inspired by Schmidt's great passion for business and business leaders. It is the entrepreneurial spirit of people like John Galardi and the leadership and principles displayed by JR Galardi that allow small businesses to thrive and make this country great.

DI ANGELO PUBLICATIONS
A Modernized Publishing Firm